Also by Michael Holzman

Lukács's Road to God

Writing as Social Action (with Marilyn Cooper)

James Jesus Angleton:
The CIA, and the Craft of Counterintelligence

Transgressions (novel)

Guy Burgess: Revolutionary in an Old School Tie

The Black Poverty Cycle and How to End It

Chelmsford Press   Briarcliff Manor, New York

"To be a poor man is hard, but to be a poor race in a land of dollars is the very bottom of hardships." W. E. B. Du Bois

Chelmsford Press
Briarcliff Manor, New York
ISBN-13: 978-1481877985
ISBN-10: 1481877984

For Rosa A. Smith

Acknowledgments

Rosa Smith, then President of the Schott Foundation for Public Education, encouraged my first explorations of these issues. Her successor, John H. Jackson, President and CEO of the Foundation, and Greg Jobin-Leeds, Chairman of the Board of the Foundation, have been endlessly supportive. Amrit Thapa has been kind enough to make his statistical expertise available whenever asked. Elaine Gross, Damon Hewitt, Phillip Jackson, Henry Levin, Cassandra Schwerner, Anthony Simmons, Elspeth Stuckey Smith, Michael Smith and Sherley Anne Williams have all been helpful and inspirational.

Jane MacKillop has been essential.

Errors are, of course, my own. I would be grateful to have them brought to my attention so that they might be corrected.

Table of Contents

Introduction

I decided to go East and learn the bond business. Everybody I knew was in the bond business, so I supposed it could support one more single man . . . Father agreed to finance me for a year, and after various delays I came East, permanently, I thought, in the spring of twenty-two ... The practical thing was to find rooms in the city, but it was a warm season, and I had just left a country of wide lawns and friendly trees, so when a young man at the office suggested that we take a house together in a commuting town, it sounded like a great idea. F. Scott Fitzgerald, *The Great Gatsby*.

Fitzgerald starts the machinery of *Gatsby*, like the scriptwriter he would become, expertly placing his narrator in the middle of the early-twentieth-century life with which he was as familiar as a tropical fish with the water in its bowl. A century later many of us still think of America as a country of wide lawns and friendly trees, a country where everybody we know is in the bond business or the real estate business or the teaching or medicine or law business and where fathers agree to finance their children while they learn those things that they will need to know in their businesses. Those children meet one another at Northwestern or Berkeley, Cornell or Yale, marry, have children themselves and bring them up in ranch or craftsman houses in Ithaca or Athens, Encino or Brookline or some commuting town near Chicago or New York. *Those* children spend a year or two with weekly visits to the doctor and hourly instruction from their parents ("Do you want that? What is it called? It's a truck!") then begin to go to classes, at first a few hours then a few days a week, arriving at kindergarten with vocabularies and socialization just right to make their eventual M.B.A., Ph.D., law or medical degree, inevitable.

That picture is true for perhaps ten percent of the country. Life for most Americans is much less, and becoming even less, comfortable. Life for nearly all — or, to be precise, 96% — of African-Americans is nothing like that.

This book is about how three different facts of life for African-Americans are intertwined and mutually reinforcing: lack of educational opportunities, poverty, and mass incarceration. All three are rooted in the historic racial prejudices of White America. Together they immobilize the great majority of African-Americans at the bottom of the income and wealth scales: below, rather than within, the increasingly stratified class system in which other Americans live. Finally, this book is about how to use the very connections among these facts of life to change them and thus improve the lives of African-Americans and with them the lives of all Americans.

Mass Incarceration

It is highly unlikely that a college educated White, non-Hispanic, American has any relatives, friends or neighbors who have been in prison. The national incarceration rate for all Whites, according to the Bureau of Justice Statistics, is 412 per 100,000 men, women and children: four-tenths of one percent. The national incarceration rate for African-Americans is more than five times as high: 2,290. The Black incarceration rate in Wisconsin, for example, is nearly twice that, 4,416 per 100,000 (415 for Whites). In Iowa it is 4,200 (309 for Whites). In the former slave states and in segregated urban neighborhoods (and most urban neighborhoods are becoming ever more segregated), it is highly unlikely that the average African-American *does not* have any relatives, friends, or neighbors who have been in prison. These disparities, it will be shown in these pages, are rooted in poverty, inadequately funded school

2

and the operations and effects of the criminal justice system and not in any extraordinary level of Black criminality.

Poverty

The average African-American family with a single income and two or three children, lives just above the line that would qualify those children for a reduced price school lunch. Half way through the depression that began in 2008, the poverty rate for the White population was 14%, while more than one-third of the Black population was in poverty. In Indiana the Black poverty rate was 49%, in Minnesota and the state of Washington, 48%. (In Minnesota the White poverty rate was 10%; in Washington the White poverty rate was 12%.)[*] Most Black families have incomes placing them in the bottom fifth of the nation's income distribution; very few rise to higher levels than those reached by their parents; and a statistically insignificant number receive incomes or accumulate wealth placing them in the top quintile, that country of wide lawns and friendly trees.

Educational Achievement

More than three-quarters of Black men do not have the education increasingly required for middle class life. Just twelve percent of Black men have Bachelor's degrees and five percent have graduate degrees. These are, respectively, just over one-third and less than half of the attainment rates for non-Hispanic White men. Five percent of the nation's Black men over the age of 25 (half of the clichéd "talented tenth") cannot provide the doctors and lawyers, professors and business leaders needed if African-Americans are to take a leadership position in the larger society. Five percent will not be a significant presence in the upper-middle class neighborhoods that are served by the best public schools.

And so, because of America's local property-tax-based system of school funding, most, perhaps 90% of African-

---

[*] Data for 2010 from the Kaiser Family Foundation.

American students attend poorly resourced schools. As a consequence, on the Grade 8 National Assessment of Educational Progress ("NAEP") Reading assessment, 90% of male Black students do not read at grade level. Only 2% score at the Advanced level in Mathematics, as compared to 35% and 12%, respectively, for White, non-Hispanic, males. On the 2011 Grade 8 NAEP Science examination, so few male Black students scored at the Advanced level that their number "rounded to zero." It is no surprise then that just over half of the male Black students in 9th grade graduate with regular diplomas four years later, as compared to three-quarters of male White, non-Hispanic, students.

The sum of these factors—mass incarceration, intergenerational poverty and a lack of educational opportunity—is a continuing catastrophe for the increasingly isolated African-American community. It is a catastrophe deeply rooted both in American history and firmly embedded in the structures of society today.

There are many voices proclaiming that the problems facing Black males are in effect either of their own making or are beyond solution. At least since Daniel Patrick Moynihan's 1965 report certain voices have attributed the achievement gap in education to the structure of the Black family. Apparently what is meant is that many Black children live in families that differ from some perceived norm in crucial ways, such as the gender of the head of the household (female) and her marital status (unmarried). Some say that the problems facing African-Americans are simply the result of a cycle of poverty endemic to ("to be expected of") a group in which two-parent families are becoming rare. This argument is often extended to include street manners and *mores*, taste in popular music and clothing and so forth. Some of those voices say those problems are a matter of attitude or character (including the semi-mythical "reluctance to act White"[1]). Some say the source of those problems is an anti-social youth culture.

On the other hand, in the introduction to *An American Dilemma: The Negro Problem and Modern Democracy* by the Swedish sociologist Gunnar Myrdal and his research team— that great monument to the study of race in America as it was just before the Civil Rights Movement—Myrdal recalled that "When the present investigator started his inquiry, his preconception was that it had to be focused on the Negro people and their peculiarities . . .

> But as he proceeded in his studies into the Negro problem, it became increasingly evident that little, if anything, could be scientifically explained in terms of the peculiarities of the Negroes themselves . . . practically all the economic, social, and political power is held by whites . . . *It is thus the white majority group that naturally determines the Negro's 'place.'*[2] (Emphasis added.)

It is good to keep this observation in mind. The "Negro Problem," as Myrdal called it, was—and is—a problem created by, maintained, and ultimately solvable only by the actions of the State, dominated as it is by the White majority, and not by Black youth or the Black community as a whole and certainly not by the Black community alone.

The range of problems facing Black males, including those problems arising from and leading to childhood poverty, are, to some large extent, the product of public policy decisions. These are not decisions made by Black children. These are not decisions made by young adult Black men who have not graduated from high school. They are, by and large, decisions made by school administrators, police, district attorneys, judges, legislators. The most dramatic and far-ranging of those decisions occur along the track of an intergenerational circuit flowing from prisons to poverty to poorly-resourced schools and back to prisons.

In order to properly trace those public policy decisions, and their effects—and what might be done to create better opportunities in life for Black males—rather than beginning as is usually done, chronologically, with the neighborhood, family type and income level into which many Black male children are born, we will begin with the involvement of young adult Black males with the police, courts and prison system.

Notes

[1] Harris, Angel L. Kids Don't Want to Fail: Oppositional Culture and the Black-White Achievement Gap. Cambridge, Massachusetts: Harvard University Press, 2011.

[2] Myrdal, Gunnar. An American Dilemma: The Negro Problem and Modern Democracy. New York: Harper & Brothers Publishers, 1944, p. li.

The Black Poverty Cycle and How to End It

Chapter I

Mass Incarceration

I think of the growth of the penal system not so much as a manifestation of discrimination, but as ... an institutionalization of racial hierarchy and the law, which is color-blind on its face, has been written and enforced in such a way that it imposed a massively disparate burden on African-Americans, particularly those with little schooling. Bruce Western[1]

The mission of the United States Department of Justice is: "To enforce the law and defend the interests of the United States according to the law; to ensure public safety against threats foreign and domestic; to provide federal leadership in preventing and controlling crime; to seek just punishment for those guilty of unlawful behavior; and *to ensure fair and impartial administration of justice for all Americans*."[2] The state attorneys general have similar missions. If White Americans have problems with the American criminal justice system, those problems are not often personal. Some think the criminal justice system is "not tough enough on crime." Others think that it is not tough enough on Wall Street. But these are usually simply theoretical concerns. In the country of wide lawns and friendly trees it is usually possible to believe that the police and the other components of the criminal justice system are really there "to serve and protect." And yet, the primary effect of the American criminal justice system on African-Americans is to remove an extraordinary proportion of working age Black men from their com-munities, impoverishing their families and those communities, condemning their children to inferior schools where they will be prepared for little other than prison. This complex of factors perpetuates a caste-like system of immobilized intergenerational poverty for African-Americans.

America is still overwhelmingly White: 78% according to the 2010 census. The ratio between African-Americans and White Americans in the general population is either six- or five-to-one, depending on how Hispanics are classified. That ratio is quite different in the prisons, where there are over 800,000 adult Black males as compared to just over a million adult White, non-Hispanic, males. In other words, there are at least four times as many African-Americans imprisoned than would be expected from their share in the general population. Although Texas and California, which are notable for mass incarceration, imprison many more White, non-Hispanics, than African-Americans, Florida—which is also notable for extraordinary mass incarceration —imprisons approximately the same number of African-Americans as White, non-Hispanics, and Georgia, New York state, Pennsylvania, Louisiana, Illinois, Virginia and North Carolina imprison more African-Americans than White, non-Hispanics, despite the fact that White, non-Hispanics, are very much in the majority in each of those states.

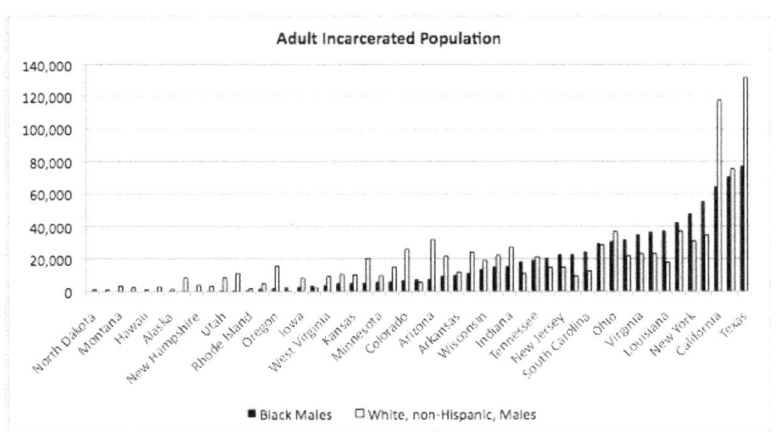

2010 Census Summary File 1: Pct 22a & B: Group Quarters Population by Sex by Group Quarters Type for the Population 18 Years and Over (White & Black Alone)

The disproportionate incarceration rate of Black men is integral to the American system of continued subordination of the descendents of enslaved Africans. That subordination, which Gunnar Myrdal and some of his contemporaries described as a *caste* system, continues to mock our ideals and frustrate our aspirations. It has been integral to the structure of our society from the beginning. It has become common the last few years, but still morally shocking, to consider the paradox of Thomas Jefferson in his beautiful house, his beautiful mind a repository of Enlightenment learning and neo-classical diagrams, living in the midst of slaves, many of whom were his own children. "We hold these truths to be self-evident, that all men are created equal, that they are endowed by their Creator with certain unalienable Rights, that among these are Life, Liberty and the pursuit of Happiness ..." So he wrote as, year after year, he enslaved, kept as slaves, his own children. He and many other Founders traded in people as if they were simply commodities: as they were. One can imagine— one cannot imagine—the scenes that took place as men sold their children in the town marketplace. That this was a moral problem did in fact occur to Jefferson: "Indeed", he wrote in his Notes on Virginia, "I tremble for my country when I reflect that God is just; that His justice cannot sleep forever."

The institution of slavery was not unique to the United States. There were slaves in China, most of whom were Chinese; there were (and still are) slaves in North Africa, some African, some of whom were European and some White Americans. The Marines, we recall, were sent—by Jefferson—to "the shores of Tripoli" to free the latter. There had been European slaves in Virginia, but these had soon enough been replaced by Africans. What catches our attention is the eventual identification of slavery in the United States *solely* with Africans and their descendents. It came to be assumed in the United States that slaves were Africans—and, to a great extent, visa versa. (According to Professor Becky Pettit, "Prior to the abolishment of slavery ... Although not all black Americans were slaves, evidence suggests that Census enumerators often miscategorized free blacks as slaves." [3]) For many White Americans, particularly in the South, this identification was so complete that it became inconceivable that African-Americans could have a civil existence that was not that of a subordinate caste. According to George Fitzhugh, a leading Southern apologist for slavery, "As a general and abstract question, negro slavery has no other claims over other forms of slavery, except that from inferiority, or rather peculiarity, of race, almost all negroes require masters."[4] The masters, in return, benefitted from, believed that they required, the unpaid labor of the slaves. A fair enough exchange, the George Fitzhughs of this world would have thought: slavery for Black men; profits for Whites.

This ideology and its profits underlay the continuing efforts to maintain a race-based system of subordination long after legal eman-cipation. The abortive revolution called Reconstruction threatened this system, but Reconstruction ended in 1876 with the withdrawal of the United States Army from the South. Although there were for the next twenty years a scattering of Black elected officials in the South, African-Americans in those states were nearly totally disenfranchised by the end of the nineteenth century, not to be able to participate in American democracy again until the 1960s. W. E. B. Du Bois observed in 1935 that "In the former slave states, from Virginia to Texas, excepting Missouri, there are no Negro state officials; no Negro members of legislatures; no judges on the bench; and usually no jurors. There are no colored county officials of any sort. In the towns and cities, there are no colored administrative officers, no members of the city councils, no magistrates, no constables and very seldom even a policeman."[5] Control of the police, the courts, the prisons and the legislatures of the South were the prerogatives of White men. As a result, Du Bois wrote, the "police courts and magistrates' courts [under Jim Crow] were in the hands of a wretched set of white Negro-hating politicians, and nine-tenths of the Negro court cases ended here and filled the chain-gangs with Negroes ... It was the policy of the state to keep the Negro laborer poor, to confine him as far as possible to menial occupations, to make him a surplus labor reservoir and to force him into peonage and unpaid toil."[6]

At any time between the end of Reconstruction and the Truman administration, a Black man, arrested on any pretext or no pretext at all by a White sheriff, brought before a White judge or a White notary public, could be charged, swiftly convicted and more or less inevitably punished with a fine carefully calculated to be beyond his means to pay. A White farmer or business man, happening to be nearby, would pay the fine, thus securing the labor of the Black man in return for this debt, which, in the way of such things, would rarely be allowed to be paid off. It was this "debt peonage" that Douglas Blackmon calls "slavery by another name." In 1908, the then-U.S. Assistant Attorney General, Charles Russell, wrote: "I have no doubt from my investigations and experiences that the chief support of peonage is the peculiar system of State laws prevailing in the South, intended evidently to compel services on the part of the working man ... it is difficult to draw a distinction between the condition of a man who remains in service against his will, because the State has passed a certain law under which he can be arrested and returned to work, and the condition of a man on a nearby farm who is actually made to stay at work by arrest and actual threats of force under the same law."[7] Debt peonage prevailed unchallenged across the South until 1942, when Attorney General Francis Biddle brought a case under the Slavery Kidnapping Act. It took nearly another decade to end such legal involuntary servitude. While slavery was abolished in the British Empire in 1833, to hold a person in slavery became a crime in the United States not in 1865, but in 1951.[8] Between those dates, African-Americans could, and often were, enslaved by means of the operations of the criminal justice system. The 1871 Virginia Supreme Court decision in the case of *Ruffin v. Commonwealth* held that a convict was "a slave of the State."[9] That decision stood until the 1960s.

"Slavery by another name" is what Blackmon calls "The Re-Enslavement of Black Americans from the Civil War to World War II." He centers his account around the operations of the vagrancy laws in the South at the end of the nineteenth century, epitomized by that which required "all free negroes and mulattoes over the age of eighteen" to have at all times written proof of employment or be deemed vagrants.[10] "Vagrancy," according to Blackmon, "the offense of a person not being able to prove at a given moment that he or she is employed ... was capriciously enforced by local sheriffs and constables, adjudicated by mayors and notaries public … and … was reserved almost exclusively for black men."[11] (The racialist application of laws that were on the face of it race-neutral recurs in this story). Blackmon believes that hundreds of thousands of Black men and boys (and some Black women and some White men) were held in debt peonage between the end of Reconstruction and the end of the Second World War. One effect of this was to provide quasi-slave labor for the plantations and factories of wealthy White families; another effect was the subordination of the region's Black population as a whole. If any Black person could at any moment be stopped, searched and perhaps sent off in chains to, say, a turpentine camp, then all Black people were without security in their persons.

Yet another effect was to lower the average cost of both White and free Black labor. As the labor of Black men in the fields, forests and factories of the South was obtainable at a cost close to, if not below, that necessary for bare survival, all wages, White as well as Black, were liable to being lowered in parallel. This system was maintained in the first instance by continual actual and threatened violence against African-Americans. The support of those White men who were not themselves employers of Black labor was secured not economically, by the provision of employment at fair wages, but ideologically: by the continual invocation of racial (as well as gender) superiority. As Du Bois reminded his readers in *Black Reconstruction:* "It must be remembered that the white group of laborers, while they received a low wage, were compensated in part by a sort of public and psychological wage. There were given public deference and titles of courtesy because they were white …

> The police were drawn from their ranks, and the courts, dependent upon their votes, treated them with such leniency as to encourage lawlessness. Their vote selected public officials and while this had small effect upon their economic situation, it had great effect upon their personal treatment and the deference shown them. White schoolhouses were the best in the community, and conspicuously placed, and they cost anywhere from twice to ten times as much per capita as the colored schools. The newspapers specialized on news that

flattered the poor whites and almost utterly ignored the Negro except in crime and ridicule."[12]

Economic self-interest is not an all-encompassing motivation in a racist society. In much of the South, White poverty was the price more or less gladly paid for Black subordination. The system worked. It still works today.

As in the time of the Fugitive Slave Act, when the reach of the "drivers of Negroes" legally extended across the entire country, under Jim Crow the condition of Black people in the South, and the attitudes of White Southerners, infected much of the rest of the country ideologically. In order to gain the acceptance of the North for ending Reconstruction "the South had to make Negroes into thieves, monsters and idiots" as Du Bois put it.[13] If it occurred to White observers in the North to think about Black debt peonage, the chain gangs, lynchings and other aspects of the Southern criminal justice system, they soon were provided with the explanation that there was a very high rate of criminal behavior among former slaves and their descendents and that "a firm hand"—strict enforcement of strict laws—was needed if there were not to be an epidemic of Black crime. This explanation was deemed sufficient. There was no more need for the average White American, North or South, to think about such things. They could simply watch *The Birth of a Nation.*

As it was posited that African-Americans were peculiarly likely to be violent criminals, the violent behavior of the police toward African-Americans followed—follows—as a matter of course. Myrdal observed that in the South under Jim Crow, it was "part of the policeman's philosophy that Negro criminals or suspects, or any Negro who shows signs of insubordination, should be punished bodily ... When once the beating habit has developed in a police department, it is ... difficult to stop ... Police brutality is greatest in the regions where murders are most numerous and death sentences are most frequent, which speaks against its having crime-preventing effects."[14] Myrdal found that the situation was not much different in the North: "In most Northern communities Negroes are more likely than whites to be arrested under any suspicious circumstances. They are more likely to be accorded discourteous or brutal treatment at the hands of the police than are whites. The rate of killing of Negroes by the police is high in many Northern cities …"[15] And so forth. These matters have not changed. According to the late conservative scholar William J. Stuntz, "Today, black crime is mostly governed by white judges and white politicians, and by the white voters who elect them."[16] In New York City, for example, at the beginning of the twenty-first century, a young adult African-American man expects to be stopped and publicly searched by police at least once a year and is not surprised to be arrested for trespass at his own front door. Similar, more egregious, police practices, often mortal, take place there and in every part of the country. In the South they often take place in the schools.[17]

The effect of such patterns of police behavior on African-Americans has not been such as to win their approval.

> The Negro is coming *more and more* to look upon law and justice, not as protecting safeguards, but as sources of humiliation and oppression … The laws are made by men who have absolutely no motive for treating the black people with courtesy or consideration … the accused law-breaker is tried, not by his peers, but too often by men who would rather punish ten innocent Negroes than let on guilty one escape.

The quotation is again from Du Bois, this time from *The Souls of Black Folk,* which, although published in 1903, seems familiar today, as it seemed to Myrdal a reasonable depiction of the situation in his day. A century after Du Bois's book, more than half a century after that of Myrdal, we are told that there are more arrests of African-Americans than others because African-Americans (still depicted as "thieves, monsters and idiots") live in high crime neighborhoods, which indeed they do. And, as crime statistics do not count the activities of criminals, but those of the police, the proof of this becomes the indisputable fact that there are many more arrests, stops and searches in African-American neighborhoods than elsewhere.[18] Round and around we go: there are in fact large numbers of violent crimes in poor White and poor Black neighborhoods, but police are concentrated in poor Black neighborhoods; the concentration of police produces a high number of arrests; a high number of arrests is interpreted as a higher crime rate, which justifies concentrating yet more police in poor Black neighborhoods. Which, by removing extraordinary numbers of working age Black men, is one of the factors that makes them both poor and the foci of violent crime.

We have seen that the subordination of African-Americans, their status as a subordinate caste, has its origin in slavery, as an economic phenomenon, and the association of slavery with African-Americans, as an ideological phenomenon. And we have seen that the economic importance of the subordinate caste status of African-Americans to the dominant structure of the White South was such as to lead to the rebirth of slavery as debt peonage. Even after the mid-twentieth-century abolition of this type of slavery, the ideological force of the subordinate caste status of African-Americans has been maintained not only in the South, but throughout the country. A strong theme in this ideological construction, in Du Bois's time and our own, is the association of African-Americans, especially African-American men, with criminality and therefore the acceptance of the extraordinary incarceration rate of Black men as something to be expected.

Bruce Western is perhaps the country's leading expert on the sociology of the criminal justice system. His *Punishment and Inequality in America* documents the enormous increase in incarcerations in the United States that began in the last quarter of the twentieth century, perhaps coincidentally, just after the passage of the Civil Rights Act. In the course of doing so he focuses on two aspects of that increase: that it is to a significant extent an artifact of arrests for drug offenses and that most of those arrested are young adult male African-Americans. Western does not belabor the obvious: the drug laws are manifestly irrational, designating *this* substance as dangerous, *that* as a near social necessity. The behaviors criminalized differ little, if at all from behaviors—such as the consumption of alcohol and prescription drugs—that are not similarly criminalized. (It is widely acknowledged that the harms associated with the behaviors in question are generally the consequence of the laws, rather than the result of those behaviors.) The laws create artificial scarcities, impoverish addicts and enrich gangs and foreign criminal cartels. The enforcement of those laws, and their consequences in terms of incarcerations, are not applied evenly across society. They are enforced in neighborhoods of concentrated poverty, not in those of concentrated wealth; they are enforced for unemployed young Black men in the streets of central Brooklyn and not for, say, older White women working at fashion magazines.

Western has found that the consequences of the late-twentieth-century changes in the practices of the criminal justice system for their target group—Black men—were severe. By the year 2000 12% of Black men age twenty to forty, 17% of those without a college degree and 32% of those without high school diplomas were incarcerated.[19] About the same number were on parole or probation. In some urban areas the statistics are even more dramatic. In Chicago, for example, it is said that the number of those with a felony record is equal to fifty-five percent of the black adult male population and 80 percent of the adult black male workforce.[20] While for most White, non-Hispanic, Americans, the police and courts they are most aware of are those depicted on television, in video games and in the movies, for most Black men the streets of America are those of a police state. Most White Americans may not know any White men who are (or have been) incarcerated. Nearly every Black American knows a man from their community who is or has been incarcerated. Often enough, that will be a neighbor or family member. For Black men, that incarcerated or formerly incarcerated person is as often as not himself. Western and his colleague Becky Pettit have observed that "incarceration is so disproportionately concentrated among low-skill black men that it has become a routine life event."[21]

If this seems melodramatic, consider these statistics. On June 30, 2010, the most recent date for which this data is available, 4.3% of Black American adult males were inmates held in custody in state or federal prisons or in local jails. One in ten Black men in their early thirties were incarcerated. (By way of comparison, less than one percent of White, non-Hispanic, males and less than two percent of those in their early thirties were imprisoned.)[22] An

19

additional 814,000 adult male Black Americans were on probation and 320,000 on parole.[23] At that moment, then, just under 10% of all Black males were under the control of the criminal justice system, rising, in some age groups, to one out of five. If we deduct boys 17 years of age and below and men over 55, we can estimate that of the ten million working age Black men in the general population remaining, 16% were either incarcerated, on probation or on parole in June 2010.[24] It is commonly estimated that twice that percentage will be imprisoned at some time during their lives and it is projected that up to two-thirds of all Black men born in 2001 and the years following can expect to spend time in jail, state or federal prisons.

There are more incarcerated Black males than incarcerated White males in the vast majority of the states imprisoning 20,000 or more men of either race.

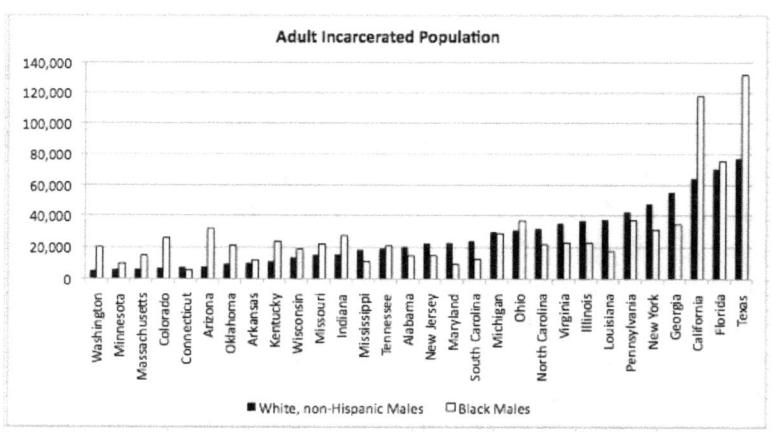

U.S. Census (2010): Table Pct22A & B: Group Quarters Population by Sex by Group Quarters Type for the Population 18 Years and Over

Looking at this graph more closely, we can note that the excess of Black over White male incarcerations in Georgia, New York state and Louisiana is particularly striking. In none of those states does the total Black population exceed one-third of the White population. The picture is quite different for incarcerated women, of whom there are 58,000 who are Black and 126,000 who are White, non-Hispanic.

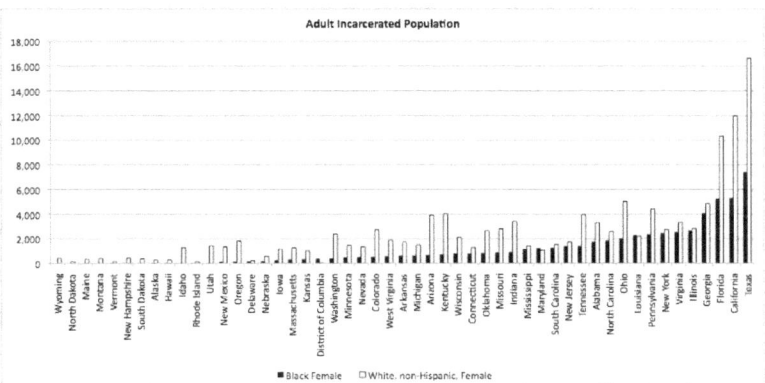

U.S. Census (2010): Table Pct22A & B: Group Quarters Population by Sex by Group Quarters Type for the Population 18 Years and Over

The incarceration rate for Black women as compared to that for White women is three times what would be expected from their respective shares in the general population, but half the degree of disproportionality of the male incarceration figures. There are only a handful of states with more incarcerated Black than White women, none of which are the mass incarceration states of Georgia, Florida, California and Texas. In other words, the comparative incarceration rates for Black and White women are inequitable, but not as egregiously so as those of Black and White men. If the incarceration proportions by race were the same for men as for women, half a million fewer Black men would have been incarcerated in 2010.

Why is that? Racism in the United States has always been gendered: few women were lynched. It was believed by slave owners that control of Black men would control the Black population. So it is still believed today. The White fear of African-American men, particularly of young adults, is a projection of that belief, operationalizing it in, among other ways, stop-and-frisk policing, trespass laws, mass incarceration, vigilante shootings.

It is well-established that incarceration rates vary with education: the more education, the less chance of incarceration. The education (or lack of education) effect is particularly strong for those who have not obtained a high school diploma. The following table shows the incarcerated young adult male Black and White populations by educational attainment in 2008.

**Men Ages Twenty to Thirty-Four, Civilian
Incarceration Rates by Educational Attainment**

Schooling	White	Black
Less than high school	12.0%	37.2%
High School	2.0	9.1
Some college	0.3	2.1
All	1.8	11.4

Adapted from: Pettit, Becky. Invisible Men.

Three times the percentage of young adult Black men as White men who had not completed high school were incarcerated in 2008; four-and-a-half times the percentage of Black as White men who *had* completed high school were in prison; seven times the percentage of Black as White men who had some college were incarcerated.

The chances that a man will be incarcerated at *some point* while a young adult similarly vary with education and race. The chances of a White man without a high school diploma being incarcerated as a young adult are nearly one in three; those for a Black man without a high school diploma are more than two in three. A diploma brings that down sharply for White men, to 6%, less sharply for Black men, to one in five. Some college brings the odds for incarceration down close to one in a hundred for White men, but, again, down only to the level for White men with a high school diploma for Black men. There seems to be a variable at work—call it Blackness—that to some extent counterbalances educational attainment as a factor in vulnerability to incarceration.

The interpretation of these statistics is complicated by two related factors. One is the common definition of the group with a high school diploma, which almost always includes those with a GED. However, the GED is not actually the equivalent of a high school diploma. The requirements are not as great and its completion, by a test or through a waiver, is not at all evidence of equivalent effort. Second, Black men, who form a disproportionate number of those receiving a GED, characteristically do so *while* in prison. According to De los Santos and Heckman: "GEDs earned while incarcerated account for as many as 20 percent of GED credentials issued to men in the US ... 68 percent of GED credentials issued to black men are likely to have been obtained while incarcerated, compared with 35 percent for Hispanic and 9 percent for white men."[25] Thus the counts of high school completion/GED among those incarcerated are doubly inflated. We should, therefore, move the GED data in regard to incarcerated Black men with high school diplomas or GEDs to the "less than high school" category, bringing the incarceration rate for the latter to perhaps 40% and that for the former to, say, 6%. The headcounts then look like this:

Male Educational Attainment for the Population 25 Years and Over

	Black	**White**
GED or no diploma	2,720,019	9,676,453
Regular high school diploma	3,062,367	16,508,194
Some college, no degree	3,119,968	14,591,029
Bachelor's degree	1,124,314	13,552,163
Graduate degree	547,473	8,286,856
Total	10,574,141	67,529,073

Sex By Educational Attainment for the Population 25 Years and Over 2008-2010 American Community Survey 3-Year Estimates.

The following chart illustrates the differences in educational attainment between Black and White men that result from reclassifying GEDs:

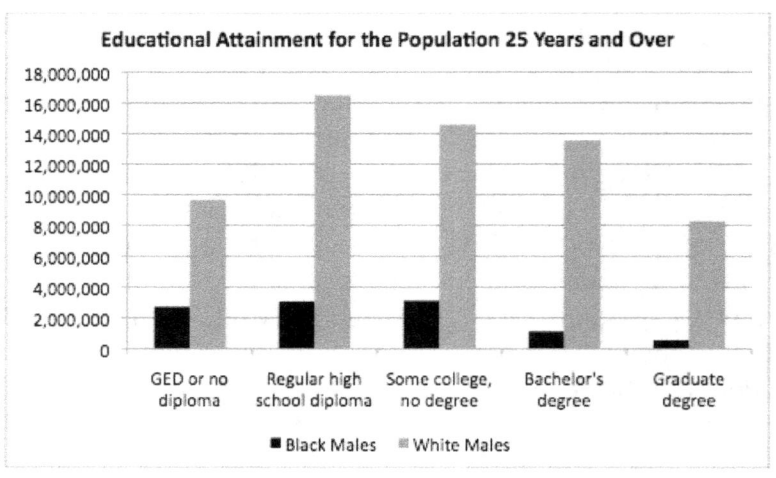

The statistics (from the U.S. Census) for White men form a close-to-normal distribution: there are approximately equal numbers of men with a GED or no diploma as with graduate degrees. The statistics for Black men are more strongly skewed to the left: it is only one-fifth as likely that a Black man will have a graduate degree as it is that he will have a GED or no diploma. We can then compare these numbers with cumulative risk of imprisonment percentages given by Pettit:

Cumulative Risk of Imprisonment by Ages 30 to 34

All		Less Than High School		High School/GED		Some College	
White	Black	White	Black	White	Black	White	Black
5.4	28.0	28.0	68.0	6.2	21.4	1.2	6.6

Adapted from Pettit, Becky. Invisible Men.

For six million of the ten and a half million young adult Black men the odds are more than two in three that they will spend time in prison. For another three million the chances are more than one in five. For only 1.6 million young adult Black men are the chances of incarceration the same as they are for young adult White men. Pettit concludes that "Spending time in prison has become more common than completing a four-year college degree or military service among young black men. And young, black, male high school dropouts are more likely to spend at least a year in prison than they are to get married. In short, among low-skill black men, spending time in prison [furthers] … their segregation from mainstream society."[26] Furthers, in fact, the segregation of impoverished Black communities as a whole from "mainstream society." Of course "impoverished Black communities" is nearly a tautology: as we will see, the vast majority of Black communities are impoverished.

Why is it that the chances of incarceration at some time between the ages of 18 and 34 for a young adult Black man are six times those of a young, non-Hispanic, White man? Why is it that this is seemingly taken for granted by (White) society at large? Hispanics in the United States occupy a socio-economic position similar to that of African-Americans: many live in poverty; many suffer from prejudice; many Hispanic children attend low-performing schools. And yet the incarceration rate for young adult Hispanic men, while twice as high as that of White, non-Hispanic, men, is only one-third that of Black men.[27] The relationship between White and Hispanic young adult male incarceration rates does not seem extreme when we take into account educational achievement, which, as we have seen, is a well-established factor affecting incarceration rates, and poverty. However, the disparity between the incarceration rates for young adult Black males and their Hispanic and other White peers cannot be explained in this way.

One interpretation of these statistics is that Black men have an extraordinary propensity to commit crimes. This is the interpretation given by representatives of the criminal justice system when explaining the concentration of police activity in Black communities. They "make Negroes into thieves, monsters and idiots," as Du Bois put it. Another interpretation is that the police have an extraordinary propensity to arrest Black men and the courts have an extraordinary propensity to incarcerate them. The latter interpretation is now sufficiently well-known in federal government circles that the United States Equal Employment Opportunity Commission (EEOC) issued "enforcement guidance" in April, 2012, on the consideration of arrest and conviction records in employment decisions.[28] The EEOC implicitly attributes these disparities in arrest and incarceration rates to disparities in enforcement of drug laws: "African-Americans and Hispanics were more likely than Whites to be arrested, convicted, or sentenced for drug offenses even though their rate of drug use is similar to the rate of drug use for Whites."[29] (As a matter of fact, the Annie E. Casey Foundation Kids Count (2012) study finds that "Among racial and ethnic groups, African-American and Asian teens were least likely (4 percent) to abuse or be dependent on alcohol or drugs" (p. 35).) If drug use rates are similar among Black, White and Hispanic Americans, and if Black and Hispanic drug users are more likely than Whites to be arrested, convicted or sentenced for drug offences, the variable, in the view of the EEOC, is not "criminality," but the operations of the police and courts.[30] The EEOC guidance document makes it clear that the Commission does not believe that most African-American men are habitual criminals in the common sense of the term. The tone and argument of the document indicate that the Commission believes, rather, that the operations of the "criminal justice system" involve systematic racially disparate effects. In effect, the federal government is stating, as if as a matter of course, that the criminal justice system often penalizes African-Americans simply for being Black.[31]

This seems indeed to be the case. As an example, we can point to New York City's "stop and frisk" activities. According to a 2007 analysis of those activities in the *Journal of the American Statistical Association*, African-Americans represented 51% of the stops while making up only 26% of the New York City population. "Blacks were stopped 23% more often than whites … *The differences in stop rates among ethnic groups are real, substantial, and not explained by previous arrest rates or precincts.*"[32] (Emphasis added). If they cannot be explained by arrest rates or precincts (i.e., "to protect the residents of high crime neighborhoods"), the residual category is to explain them by the policies and practices of the police themselves. In 2010, according to *The New York Times,* when over 50,000 people in New York City were arrested on charges of marijuana possession, more than during the entire 19-year period from 1978 to 1996, "Seventy percent of those arrested are younger than 30, and 86 percent are black or Hispanic, even though, according to the Drug Policy Group, "young whites use marijuana at higher rates."

> Possession of less than 25 grams of marijuana has been a violation, not a jailable crime, in New York since 1977. But having the drug "open to public view" is a crime, and advocates say that many people who simply have marijuana in their pockets are charged with having it in the open after officers order them to empty their pockets.[33]

As we have learned, the pockets of young White people are more likely than the pockets of young Black people to contain marijuana, but New York City police are more likely to unlawfully order young Black people to empty their pockets, and then arrest them for doing so. A 2012 study of cases in the Bronx borough of New York City by the Bronx Defenders legal assistance agency found that 40% of arrests for low-level possession in 2011 were unlawful.[34]

The total number of marijuana arrests in the United States in 2010 was 854,000.[35] Most of those were arrests of African-American and Hispanic young men. If the findings of the Bronx Defenders study are nationally applicable, and there is no reason to think that they are not, 341,000 of those were unlawful arrests. In other words, hundreds of thousands of young Black and Hispanic men are unlawfully arrested each year for purported marijuana offenses alone. To these may be added those incarcerated Black men who would not be incarcerated, or would not be incarcerated for such lengthy periods, if it were not due to the disparate effects of arrests and sentencing for crack and powder cocaine. We can calculate this disproportionality in another way as a check on at least the order of magnitude of our estimates. Between 1980 and 2009, the rate of arrests of Black adults for drug possession averaged three times that of White adults.

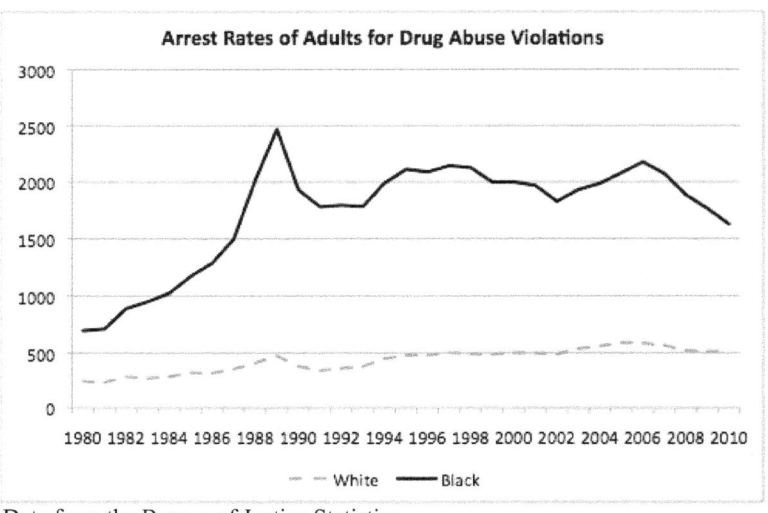

Data from the Bureau of Justice Statistics

If we calculate a projected number of adult Black drug arrests (including both possession and sales) based on the drug arrest rate for White adults (given that the actual criminalized activity is roughly equivalent), we can derive the following chart:

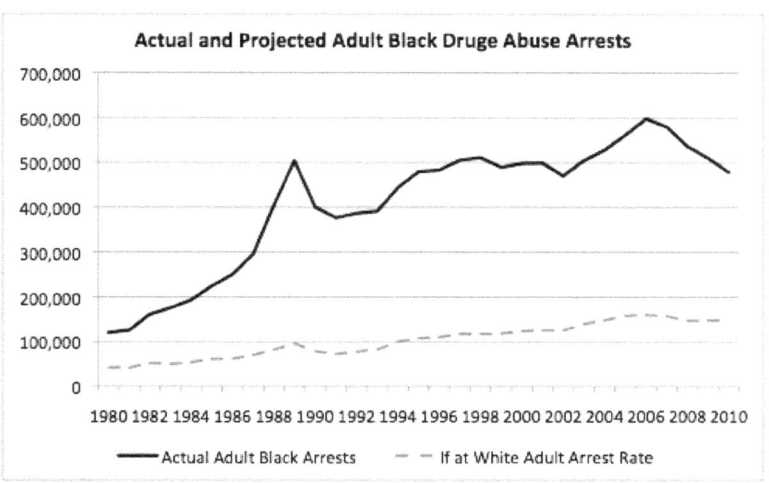

The difference between this projection and actual arrests, on average, is over 300,000 arrests of Black adults annually beyond the amount to be expected based on the actually equivalent drug use rates of Blacks and Whites. This corresponds well with the estimate of 314,000 unlawful arrests projected from the Bronx Defenders study. As the ratio between drug arrests and incarcerations is approximately three to one, there may be something on the order of 100,000 more Black adults incarcerated every year as the result of unlawful drug arrests than would be the case if the criminal justice system operated equitably. Given that the average sentence for drug offenses is about five years, at any one time it may be that hundreds of thousands of Black adults (overwhelmingly male) are in prison, away from their communities, leaving their families in poverty, because of the disproportionate number of drug arrests alone.

Andrew Hacker has pointed out a flaw in the emphasis on drug offenses as the single cause of the disproportionality of incarcerations: many more Black men with felony convictions are incarcerated for violent crimes than for drug offenses.[36] Let us turn then to an analysis of the racial distributions of violent crimes. The following table was generated for this study by Mr. Dan Bernstein of the New York State Bureau of Corrections:

TABLE 4A.   CRIME BY INMATE ETHNIC STATUS; UNDERCUSTODY POPULATION

CRIME	WHITE NUMBER	COL PCT	BLACK NUMBER	COL PCT	HISPANIC NUMBER	COL PCT	OTHER NUMBER	COL PCT	UNKNOWN NUMBER	COL PCT	TOTAL NUMBER	COL PCT
VIOLENT FELONY												
MURDER	1316	10.2%	3902	14.3%	1894	14.1%	134	14.4%	23	5.6%	7269	13.2%
ATTEMPTED MURDER	175	1.3%	756	2.8%	391	2.9%	27	2.9%	7	1.7%	1354	2.5%
MANSLT 1ST,AG 2ND	275	2.1%	1125	4.1%	694	5.2%	44	4.7%	13	3.2%	2151	3.9%
RAPE 1ST	464	3.6%	819	3.0%	417	3.1%	26	2.8%	9	2.2%	1735	3.2%
ROBBERY 1ST	490	3.8%	2745	10.1%	1078	8.0%	46	4.9%	10	2.4%	4369	8.0%
ROBBERY 2ND	434	3.4%	1823	6.7%	760	5.7%	43	4.6%	15	3.7%	3075	5.6%
ASSAULT 1ST	268	2.1%	1096	4.0%	583	4.3%	34	3.7%	10	2.4%	1991	3.6%
ASSAULT 2ND	340	2.6%	738	2.7%	405	3.0%	29	3.1%	13	3.2%	1525	2.8%
BURGLARY 1ST	243	1.9%	578	2.1%	281	2.1%	15	1.6%	5	1.2%	1122	2.0%
BURGLARY 2ND	1253	9.7%	1493	5.5%	928	6.9%	67	7.2%	27	6.6%	3768	6.9%
ARSON 1ST,2ND	90	.7%	85	.3%	30	.2%	2	.2%	0		207	.4%
SODOMY 1ST	520	4.0%	310	1.1%	228	1.7%	22	2.4%	5	1.2%	1085	2.0%
SEX AB 1ST,AG.2	574	4.5%	297	1.1%	302	2.2%	23	2.5%	7	1.7%	1203	2.2%
WEAPONS OFFENSES	222	1.7%	2466	9.1%	688	5.1%	45	4.8%	24	5.9%	3445	6.3%
KIDNAPPING 1ST,2ND	101	.8%	150	.6%	76	.6%	39	4.2%	1	.2%	367	.7%
OTHER VFO SEX OFF	205	1.6%	93	.3%	109	.8%	5	.5%	4	1.0%	416	.8%
OTHER VIOLENT	37	.3%	29	.1%	28	.2%	3	.3%	2	.5%	99	.2%
TOTAL	7005	54.3%	18505	68.0%	8892	66.2%	604	64.9%	175	42.8%	35181	64.1%
OTHER COERCIVE												
MANSLAUGHTER 2ND	113	.9%	106	.4%	68	.5%	4	.4%	3	.7%	294	.5%
OTHER HOMICIDE	97	.8%	27	.1%	25	.2%	6	.6%	1	.2%	156	.3%
ROBBERY 3RD	254	2.0%	706	2.6%	300	2.2%	21	2.3%	15	3.7%	1296	2.4%
ATT ASSAULT 2ND	112	.9%	261	1.0%	99	.7%	7	.8%	3	.7%	482	.9%
CONSPIRACY 2,3,4	51	.4%	94	.3%	121	.9%	5	.5%	4	1.0%	275	.5%
OTHER WEAPONS	107	.8%	353	1.3%	143	1.1%	10	1.1%	6	1.5%	619	1.1%
OTHER SEX OFFENSES	503	3.9%	172	.6%	87	.6%	17	1.8%	8	2.0%	787	1.4%
OTHER COERCIVE	222	1.7%	152	.6%	84	.6%	15	1.6%	2	.5%	476	.9%
TOTAL	1459	11.3%	1871	6.9%	927	6.9%	85	9.1%	43	10.5%	4385	8.0%
DRUG OFFENSES												
DRUG SALE	505	3.9%	2209	8.1%	1248	9.3%	39	4.2%	38	9.3%	4039	7.4%
DRUG POSSESSION	433	3.4%	1679	6.2%	958	7.1%	38	4.1%	32	7.8%	3140	5.7%
TOTAL	938	7.3%	3888	14.3%	2206	16.4%	77	8.3%	70	17.1%	7179	13.1%
PROPERTY AND OTHER OFFENSES												
BURGLARY 3RD	942	7.3%	755	2.8%	463	3.4%	32	3.4%	25	6.1%	2217	4.0%
GRAND LARCENY	628	4.9%	517	1.9%	246	1.8%	31	3.3%	21	5.1%	1443	2.6%
FORGERY	203	1.6%	214	.8%	60	.4%	8	.9%	9	2.2%	494	.9%
STOLEN PROPERTY	150	1.2%	162	.6%	70	.5%	7	.8%	7	1.7%	396	.7%
DRIVE INTOXICATED	693	5.4%	106	.4%	85	.6%	23	2.5%	20	4.9%	927	1.7%
CONTEMPT 1ST	168	1.3%	159	.6%	55	.4%	9	1.0%	7	1.7%	398	.7%
ALL OTHER FELONIES	477	3.7%	406	1.5%	175	1.3%	37	4.0%	25	6.1%	1120	2.0%
TOTAL	3261	25.3%	2319	8.5%	1154	8.6%	147	15.8%	114	27.9%	6995	12.7%
YO & JO												
YOUTHFUL OFFENDER	211	1.6%	506	1.9%	212	1.6%	16	1.7%	5	1.2%	950	1.7%
JUVENILE OFFENDER	18	.1%	122	.4%	40	.3%	1	.1%	2	.5%	183	.3%
TOTAL	229	1.8%	628	2.3%	252	1.9%	17	1.8%	7	1.7%	1133	2.1%
GRAND TOTAL	12892	100.0%	27211	100.0%	13431	100.0%	930	100.0%	409	100.0%	54873	100.0%

UNDERCUSTODY POPULATION ON 09-JUN-12

Summarizing the categories gives this:

Crime	White Prisoners	Percent White	Black Prisoners	Percent Black	Hispanic Prisoners	Percent Hispanic	Total
Violent Felony	7,005	20%	18,505	54%	8,892	26%	34,402
Other Coercive	1,459	34%	1,871	44%	927	22%	4,257
Drug Offenses	938	13%	3,883	55%	2,206	31%	7,027
Youth & Juvenile	229	21%	628	57%	252	23%	1,109
Total	12,892	24%	27,211	51%	13,431	25%	53,534

Half those in custody as the result of felony convictions in New York State prisons are Black and approximately equal numbers are White, non-Hispanic, and Hispanic (the total given here does not include the small numbers of "Others" and "Unknown"). The distribution in the general population in the state is 58% White, non-Hispanic, 16% Black and 18% Hispanic. Thus the Black prison population is far greater than proportionate to either the Hispanic or White, non-Hispanic, prison populations. The offenses of White, non-Hispanic, prisoners (24% of the total) are predominately crimes against property (48% of all White incarcerations) and "Other Violent Offenses" (34%): for the most part "other sexual offenses" and robbery. The offenses of Black prisoners are Violent Felonies (murder, robbery and weapons violations) and Drug Offenses.

Why are this large number of Black men in prison for violent offenses? Is there something special in Black life that causes men to murder and rob one another (as it is indeed other African-Americans who are most often the victims)? The answer seems to be "yes," and that factor is disproportionate poverty. Professor Lance Hannon, usually in collaboration with Professor Robert DeFina, both now at Villanova, has published a series of studies establishing a causal chain connecting incarceration for criminal behavior to poverty. In an article asking whether poverty's effects on violent crime varies with race, they find that in fact, this is *not* the case. They conclude: "Reductions in neighborhood poverty appear to produce similar reductions in violent crime in white and black neighborhoods."[37] And, one deduces, the reverse. Their research indicates that the higher rates of violent crime in Black neighborhoods is an effect of poverty, not race.

Jeffrey Fagan, Valerie West and Jan Holland of Columbia University found from a review of the research that the "risks of going to jail or prison grow over time for persons living in poor neighborhoods, contributing to the accumulation of social and economic adversity for people living in these areas, as well as to the [lack of] overall well-being of the neighborhood itself."[38] Fagan and his colleagues conclude from this and other analyses that "incarceration is not simply a consequence of neighborhood crime, but instead may ... actually elevate crime within neighborhoods." [39] The neighborhoods in question are those housing people, for the most part African-American people, living in poverty: "[T]he overall excess of incarceration rates over crime rates seems to be concentrated among non-white males living in the City's poorest neighborhoods ... neighborhoods with high rates of incarceration invite closer and more punitive police enforcement and parole surveillance, contributing to the growing number of repeat admissions and the resilience of incarceration, even as crime rates fall. *Incarceration begets more incarceration, and incarceration also begets more crime, which in turn invites more aggressive enforcement, which then re-supplies incarceration.* [40] [Emphasis added.] Fagan and his colleagues conclude that "incarceration provides a steady supply of offenders for more incarceration.

> We show that over a relatively long time period, and across very different levels of crime citywide and within neighborhoods, incarceration trends first unfold as closely tied to crime, and then over the interval, become somewhat independent of crime. As this cycle spirals forward, incarceration threatens to become endogenous in these neighborhoods, or "grown from within," seeping into and permanently staining the social and psychological fabric of neighborhood life in poor neighborhoods of New York and many other cities. Incarceration thus is part of the ecological backdrop of childhood socialization, whose effects are multiplied by grinding poverty, and an everyday contingency, particularly for young men, as they navigate the transition from adolescence to adulthood. As the risks of going to jail or prison grow over time for persons living in these areas, their prospects for marriage or earning a living and family sustaining wage diminish as the incarceration rates around them rise, closing off social exits into productive social roles. Overtime, incarceration creates more incarceration in a spiraling dynamic. [41]

It is important to emphasize here that Fagan and his colleagues are not saying that crime is rising in these areas, but that the criminal justice system is incarcerating increasing numbers of young men "independent of crime." This is distinguishable from Blackmon's "slavery by another name" only in that the process does not end in slave labor but in incarceration, which is an expense, not a source of income. In other words, it is a tax levied by themselves on those who control the criminal justice system. There are those who rationalize this by pointing to the rising profits of private prisons, but most prisons are governmental: their costs greatly outweigh the corporate profits of private prisons. Mass incarceration of African-American men is not dependent on the existence of corporate prisons. It is a price, an accepted cost, of an ideology of racial inferiority.

In these early decades of the twenty-first century, disparate poverty rates and rates of contacts with police, as exemplified by "stop and frisk" and other police actions, lead to (rather than from) disparate rates of arrests and these, in turn to disparate rates of incarceration. Just as vagrancy laws were used in the Jim Crow era to maintain structures of inequality and debt peonage in the South, so today drug laws and police practices not necessarily connected with those laws, remove large numbers of Black men from their communities and not incidentally, the electoral rolls. For in many, if not most cases, those convicted of a felony are literally disenfranchised. As with Jim Crow debt-peonage, today, "Once a person is labeled a felon, he or she is ushered into a parallel universe in which discrimination, stigma, and exclusion are perfectly legal, and privileges of citizenship such as voting and jury service are off-limits."[42] This variety of civic death is one consequence of mass incarceration. There are others. The more felons in a group, the more families living in poverty, the fewer voters. The fewer voters, the less influence over decisions about such matters as police practices and school funding.

In *The New Jim Crow: Mass Incarceration in the Age of Colorblindness,* Michelle Alexander asserts that "mass incarceration operates as a tightly networked system of laws, policies, customs, and institutions that operate collectively to ensure the subordinate status of a group defined largely by race."[43] She sees the operations of the criminal justice system as formative for the structure of contemporary society: "We have not ended racial caste in America; we have merely redesigned it."[44] Although it could be pedantically argued that caste is a specifically Hindu social structure, "caste" is a convenient term for any group of people with highly restricted social mobility. Many societies have pariah castes. Indian Untouchables "were" those who made their living as butchers, hunters, fishermen, leather workers and those engaged in sanitation. Japanese pariahs, the burakumin or kawata, were leather workers and undertakers.[45] In Europe the pariah groups have included Gypsies and Jews (and for some, the Irish). The *class identification* of an individual can change—a middle class person can become impoverished or, on the other hand, can marry into an aristocracy—however, caste is maintained without reference with economic status. In India, Kocheril Raman Narayanan, was an Untouchable, a Dalit, a member of a Scheduled Caste, for all that he was President of India. In the United States, it is the association between the former status of enslavement and the racial identity of Africans and their descendents that has led to the perpetuation of the status of African-Americans as something close enough to a caste to allow the use of the term. As Du Bois has taught us, an outward sign of that caste is the imputation, the imposition, of criminality: the vagrancy criminality of debt peonage under Jim Crow, the drug-offense criminality of the late-twentieth and early-twenty first centuries.

Michelle Alexander goes so far as to claim that in relation to African-Americans, "The nature of the criminal justice system has changed. It is no longer concerned primarily with the prevention and punishment of crime, but rather with the management and control of the dispossessed,"[46] with the designation and enforcement of caste. Blackmon would argue that, especially in the South, no change was needed. It could also be pointed out that criminal justice systems are always concerned with both crime and the management and control of members of subordinate groups. What Alexander has brought to wide attention is that in twenty-first-century America, in both the North and the South, increasingly the latter role—control of members of subordinate groups—predominates, in stark contrast to what Myrdal hoped from democracy, which he idealistically called "the American Creed." Alexander argues that this co-option of policing, courts and prisons has as its primary purpose the maintenance of the American caste system. "Today mass incarceration defines the meaning of blackness in America: black people, especially black men, are criminals. That is what it means to be black …"[47] Perhaps what *has* changed is exactly this penetration of traditional

Southern ideas of the purpose of the criminal justice system throughout the country as a whole. Never were the Fugitive Slave Laws embraced so warmly outside the South as is the agenda of "law and order" today.

Alexander's argument moves from the unusual nature of the crimes which are the focus of the "war on drugs," to the disproportionate and extraordinary scale of incarceration in this country, and then to the resultant construction, reconstruction, of caste. "The process of marking black youth *as* black criminals is essential to the function of mass incarceration as [constitutive of] a racial caste system."[48] More than three-quarters of a century ago Du Bois wrote that "The normal amount of crime which an ignorant working population would have evolved has been tremendously increased [by the Southern criminal justice system]. Young criminals and vagrants were deliberately multiplied and this in turn made an excuse for mob law and lynching."[49] As researchers Bruce Western and Becky Pettit have pointed out, these disparate rates of incarceration are a matter of implicit public policy: "The United States' prison population did not balloon by accident, *nor was its expansion driven principally by surging crime rates or demographic dynamics beyond the control of state leaders.* Rather, the growth flowed primarily from changes in sentencing laws, inmate release decisions, community supervision practices and other correctional policies that determine who goes to prison and for how long."[50] [Emphasis added.]

What is to be done? The answer is still that with which Myrdal concluded his discussion of the criminal justice system in the South, circa 1940: "White people must be taught to understand the damaging effects upon the whole society of a system of justice which is not equitable."[51] Mass incarceration could be brought to an end in an afternoon. Local district attorneys and police chiefs could make the decision to stop inequitable arrests and prosecutions any day over lunch. They could issue the requisite orders when they returned to their offices and announce them to the press later in the afternoon.

We can put down a marker here: 100,000 young adult Black men imprisoned each year under the drug laws who most probably would not have been imprisoned if they were White. Many times that number imprisoned for violent offenses arising from the sheer poverty endemic in Black neighborhoods. These point us toward a more detailed discussion of African-American poverty and then to public education and Black male students. They point also to a way out of the circuit of mass incarceration, poverty and inadequate education.

Appendix to Chapter I

TABLE I

Incarcerated Males 18 Years and Over by Race: 2010

Sorted by State

State	Black			White, non-Hispanic		
	Incarcerated	Rate per 100,000	Percentage Incarcerated	Incarcerated	Rate per 100,000	Percentage Incarcerated
Alabama	20,508	5,033	5%	14,746	1,216	1%
Alaska	267	3,002	3%	1,507	844	1%
Arizona	7,475	7,901	8%	31,793	2,160	2%
Arkansas	10,262	6,858	7%	12,076	1,464	1%
California	64,392	7,925	8%	117,801	1,942	2%
Colorado	6,811	9,250	9%	25,864	1,880	2%
Connecticut	7,379	6,096	6%	5,812	596	1%
Delaware	3,649	5,841	6%	2,291	1,010	1%
District of Columbia	2,734	2,574	3%	158	169	0%
Florida	70,619	7,101	7%	75,426	1,725	2%
Georgia	55,311	5,819	6%	34,387	1,690	2%
Hawaii	194	2,705	3%	1,112	863	1%
Idaho	287	-	-	8,477	1,743	2%
Illinois	36,662	6,113	6%	22,956	729	1%
Indiana	15,582	8,159	8%	27,270	1,374	1%
Iowa	2,829	9,307	9%	8,387	818	1%
Kansas	5,182	8,921	9%	10,311	1,236	1%
Kentucky	11,240	9,997	10%	23,800	1,702	2%
Louisiana	37,335	7,886	8%	17,679	1,702	2%
Maine	234	-	-	2,971	613	1%
Maryland	22,937	4,057	4%	9,655	801	1%
Massachusetts	6,130	4,026	4%	14,931	777	1%
Michigan	29,482	6,397	6%	28,608	988	1%
Minnesota	5,861	6,413	6%	9,850	581	1%
Mississippi	18,338	5,178	5%	11,265	1,737	2%
Missouri	15,225	6,727	7%	22,125	1,212	1%
Montana	133	-	-	3,348	977	1%
Nebraska	1,842	6,675	7%	4,782	844	1%
Nevada	5,180	6,608	7%	10,653	1,765	2%

New Hampshire	318	-	-	3,848	822	1%
New Jersey	22,602	5,663	6%	14,817	747	1%
New Mexico	986	5,649	6%	11,275	3,335	3%
New York	47,754	4,748	5%	30,906	709	1%
North Carolina	31,747	4,768	5%	21,809	933	1%
North Dakota	124	-	-	1,387	584	1%
Ohio	30,735	6,565	7%	36,617	1,037	1%
Oklahoma	9,643	10,309	10%	21,386	2,163	2%
Oregon	2,058	7,279	7%	15,572	1,319	1%
Pennsylvania	42,384	9,268	9%	36,962	948	1%
Rhode Island	1,086	5,372	5%	1,842	593	1%
South Carolina	24,156	5,668	6%	12,551	1,113	1%
South Dakota	454	-	-	3,340	1,268	1%
Tennessee	19,200	5,549	6%	21,097	1,162	1%
Texas	77,251	7,828	8%	131,990	3,000	3%
Utah	737	6,792	7%	8,515	1,100	1%
Vermont	124	-	-	1,212	527	1%
Virginia	34,945	6,586	7%	22,883	1,170	1%
Washington	5,276	5,882	6%	20,276	1,065	1%
West Virginia	4,061	16,246	16%	9,323	1,401	1%
Wisconsin	13,604	12,190	12%	18,959	1,030	1%
Wyoming	140	-	-	2,493	1,318	1%

PCT22B: Group Quarters Population by Sex by Group Quarters Type for the Population 18 Year and Over. 2010 Census Summary File 1.

TABLE 2

Incarcerated Males 18 Years and Over by Race: 2010

Sorted by Black Male Incarceration Rates

State	Black			White, non-Hispanic		
	Incarcerated	Rate per 100,000	%	Incarcerated	Rate per 100,000	%
West Virginia	4,061	16,246	16%	9,323	1,401	1%
Wisconsin	13,604	12,190	12%	18,959	1,030	1%
Oklahoma	9,643	10,309	10%	21,386	2,163	2%
Kentucky	11,240	9,997	10%	23,800	1,702	2%
Iowa	2,829	9,307	9%	8,387	818	1%
Pennsylvania	42,384	9,268	9%	36,962	948	1%
Colorado	6,811	9,250	9%	25,864	1,880	2%
Kansas	5,182	8,921	9%	10,311	1,236	1%
Indiana	15,582	8,159	8%	27,270	1,374	1%
California	64,392	7,925	8%	117,801	1,942	2%
Arizona	7,475	7,901	8%	31,793	2,160	2%
Louisiana	37,335	7,886	8%	17,679	1,702	2%
Texas	77,251	7,828	8%	131,990	3,000	3%
Oregon	2,058	7,279	7%	15,572	1,319	1%
Florida	70,619	7,101	7%	75,426	1,725	2%
Arkansas	10,262	6,858	7%	12,076	1,464	1%
Utah	737	6,792	7%	8,515	1,100	1%
Missouri	15,225	6,727	7%	22,125	1,212	1%
Nebraska	1,842	6,675	7%	4,782	844	1%
Nevada	5,180	6,608	7%	10,653	1,765	2%
Virginia	34,945	6,586	7%	22,883	1,170	1%
Ohio	30,735	6,565	7%	36,617	1,037	1%
Minnesota	5,861	6,413	6%	9,850	581	1%
Michigan	29,482	6,397	6%	28,608	988	1%
Illinois	36,662	6,113	6%	22,956	729	1%
Connecticut	7,379	6,096	6%	5,812	596	1%
Washington	5,276	5,882	6%	20,276	1,065	1%
Delaware	3,649	5,841	6%	2,291	1,010	1%
Georgia	55,311	5,819	6%	34,387	1,690	2%
South	24,156	5,668	6%	12,551	1,113	1%

Carolina						
New Jersey	22,602	5,663	6%	14,817	747	1%
New Mexico	986	5,649	6%	11,275	3,335	3%
Tennessee	19,200	5,549	6%	21,097	1,162	1%
Rhode Island	1,086	5,372	5%	1,842	593	1%
Mississippi	18,338	5,178	5%	11,265	1,737	2%
Alabama	20,508	5,033	5%	14,746	1,216	1%
North Carolina	31,747	4,768	5%	21,809	933	1%
New York	47,754	4,748	5%	30,906	709	1%
Maryland	22,937	4,057	4%	9,655	801	1%
Massachusetts	6,130	4,026	4%	14,931	777	1%
Alaska	267	3,002	3%	1,507	844	1%
Hawaii	194	2,705	3%	1,112	863	1%
District of Columbia	2,734	2,574	3%	158	169	0%
Idaho	287	-	-	8,477	1,743	2%
Maine	234	-	-	2,971	613	1%
Montana	133	-	-	3,348	977	1%
New Hampshire	318	-	-	3,848	822	1%
North Dakota	124	-	-	1,387	584	1%
South Dakota	454	-	-	3,340	1,268	1%
Vermont	124	-	-	1,212	527	1%
Wyoming	140	-	-	2,493	1,318	1%

PCT22B: Group Quarters Population by Sex by Group Quarters Type for the Population 18 Year and Over. 2010 Census Summary File 1.

Notes

[1] Western, Bruce. "Interview with Bruce Western." Social Thought and Research, Volume 30 (2009). http://hdl.handle.net/1808/5697

[2] http://www.justice.gov/about/about.html

[3] Pettit, Becky. Invisible Men: Mass Incarceration and the Myth of Black Progress. New York: Russell Sage Foundation, 2011, p. 23.

[4] Fitzhugh, George. The Blessings of Slavery in http://www.teachingamericanhistory.org/library/index.asp?documentprint=2597

[5] Du Bois, Black Reconstruction in America, 1860-1880. New York: Free Press, 1999, p. 694.

[6] Du Bois, p. 696.

[7] Quoted in Du Bois,p. 696,

[8] Blackmon, Douglas A. Slavery by Another Name: The Re-Enslavement of Black Americans from the Civil War to World War II. New York: Doubleday, 2008, p. 381.

[9] Alexander, Michelle. The New Jim Crow: Mass Incarceration in the Age of Colorblindness. The New Press: New York, 2010, p. 31.

[10] Alexander, p. 28.

[11] Blackmon, p. 1.

[12] Du Bois, pp. 700-1.

[13] Du Bois, p. 679.

[14] Myrdal, Gunnar. An American Dilemma: The Negro Problem and Modern Democracy. New York: Harper & Brothers Publishers, 1944, p. 541.

[15] Myrdal, p. 527.

[16] Stuntz, William J. The Collapse of American Criminal Justice. Harvard University Press, 2011, p. 61.

[17] Rivera, Ray. "Pockets of City See Higher Use of Force During Police Stops." The New York Times, August 16, 2012 and Associated Press. "U.S. Justice Department Alleges Violations of Students' Rights in Meridian, Miss., Schools." The Times-Picayune, August 10, 2012.

[18] " . . . research has convincingly demonstrated a significant disconnect between crime rates and incarceration rates . . . even as crime rates have fallen, the size of the penal population has increased. . ." Pettit, p. 39.

[19] Western, Bruce. Punishment and Inequality in America. New York: Russell Sage Foundation, 2006, pp. 16-7.

[20] Alexander, p. 184.

[21] Pettit, p. 5.

[22] Glaze, Lauren E. Correctional Population in the United States, 2010. U.S. Department of Justice, Office of Justice Programs, Bureau of Justice Statistics, December 2011, NCJ 236319.

[23] Glaze, Lauren E. and Bonczar, Thomas P. Probation and Parole in the United States, 2010. U.S. Department of Justice, Office of Justice Programs, Bureau of Justice Statistics, November 2011, NCJ 236019.

[24] By way of comparison, according to J. Arch Getty and his colleagues, the population of the Soviet Gulag peaked at 1.7 million 1953. As the population of the Soviet Union at that time was approximately 180 million, less than 1% of the total, perhaps two or three percent of the adult population were in the camps.

[25] De los Santos, Barbur I. and Heckman, James J. Prevalence of Prison GED Recipiency and Implications for Labor Market Outcomes and Recividism. May 11, 2005

[26] Pettit, p. 18.

[27] White: 1.8%; Black: 11.4%; Hispanic: 3.7% (Western and Pettit, op.cit.).

[28] Consideration of Arrest and Conviction Records in Employment Decisions Under Title VII of the Civil Rights Act of 1964. See: www.eeoc.gov/laws/guidance/arrest_conviction.cfm#sdendnote65sym

[29] See, e.g., Human Rights Watch, Decades of Disparity: Drug Arrests and Race in the United States 1 (2009), http://www.hrw.org/sites/default/files/reports/us0309web_1.pdf (noting that the "[t]he higher rates of black drug arrests do not reflect higher rates of black drug offending . . . . blacks and whites engage in drug offenses - possession and sales - at roughly comparable rates"); Substance Abuse & Mental Health Servs. Admin., U.S. Dep't of Health & Human Servs., Results from the 2010 National Survey on Drug Use and Health: Summary of National Findings 21 (2011), http://oas.samhsa.gov/NSDUH/2k10NSDUH/2k10Results.pdf (reporting that in 2010, the rates of illicit drug use in the United States among persons aged 12 or older were 10.7% for African-Americans, 9.1% for Whites, and 8.1% for Hispanics); Harry Levine & Deborah Small, N.Y. Civil Liberties Union, Marijuana Arrest Crusade: Racial Bias and Police Policy In New York City, 1997""2007, at 13""16 (2008), www.nyclu.org/files/MARIJUANA-ARREST-CRUSADE_Final.pdf (citing U.S. Government surveys showing that Whites use marijuana at higher rates than African-Americans and Hispanics; however, the marijuana arrest rate of Hispanics is nearly

three times the arrest rate of Whites, and the marijuana arrest rate of African-Americans is five times the arrest rate of Whites).

[30] The EEOC follows the common practice of using "Blacks and Hispanics" as a single category for rhetorical purposes, even when, as here, it would be better to consider them separately.

[31] The EEOC is concerned that employers, using the mere fact of a prior record of arrest and/or conviction to screen out job applicants, will by so doing screen out disproportionate numbers of minority, especially Black, applicants. The guidance states that:

- An employer's use of an individual's criminal history in making employment decisions may, in some instances, violate the prohibition against employment discrimination under Title VII of the Civil Rights Act of 1964, as amended . . .
- An employer's neutral policy (e.g., excluding applicants from employment based on certain criminal conduct) may disproportionately impact some individuals protected under Title VII, and may violate the law if not job related and consistent with business necessity (disparate impact liability).

The EEOC then states that these conclusions are based on the fact that "National data supports a finding that criminal record exclusions have a disparate impact based on race and national origin." By way of background, the guidance notes that:

> In the last twenty years, there has been a significant increase in the number of Americans who have had contact with the criminal justice system and, concomitantly, a major increase in the number of people with criminal records in the working-age population. In 1991, only 1.8% of the adult population had served time in prison. After ten years, in 2001, the percentage rose to 2.7% (1 in 37 adults).[7] By the end of 2007, 3.2% of all adults in the United States (1 in every 31) were under some form of correctional control involving probation, parole, prison, or jail. The Department of Justice's Bureau of Justice Statistics (DOJ/BJS) has concluded that, if incarceration rates do not decrease, approximately 6.6% of all persons born in the United States in 2001 will serve time in state or federal prison during their lifetimes.

> Arrest and incarceration rates are particularly high for African-American and Hispanic men . . . Assuming that current incarceration rates remain unchanged, about 1 in 17

White men are expected to serve time in prison during their lifetime; by contrast, this rate climbs to 1 in 6 for Hispanic men; and to 1 in 3 for African-American men.

It follows that if overall incarceration rates continue to increase as predicted, most African-American men (2 in 3) will be expected to serve time in prison.

[32] Gelman, Andrew, Fagan, Jeffrey, and Alex Kiss. An Analysis of the New York City Police Department's "Stop-and-Frisk" Policy in the Context of Claims of Racial Bias. Journal of the American Statistical Association September 2007, Vol. 102, No. 479, Applications and Case Studies.

[33] Speri, Alice. "2010 Marijuana Arrests Top 1978-96 Total," New York Times, February 11, 2011.

[34] Editorial. "Examining Marijuana Arrests," The New York Times, April 1, 2012.

[35] "Crime in the United States 2010," FBI Uniform Crime Report (Washington, DC: US Dept. of Justice, September 2011), Table 29. http://www.fbi.gov/about-us/cjis/ucr/crime-in-the-u.s/2010/crime-in-the-...

[36] Private conversation.

[37] Hannon, Lance and Robert DeFina. "Violent Crime In African-American And White Neighborhoods: Is Poverty's Detrimental Effect Race-Specific?" http://www88.homepage.villanova.edu/lance.hannon/Forthcoming%20in%20the%20Journal%20of%20Poverty.pdf accessed 06/15/12

[38] Fagan, Jeffrey, Valerie West, and Jan Holland. Reciprocal Effects of Crime and Incarceration in New York City Neighborhoods. Fordham Urban Law Journal, Volume 30, Issue 5, 2002, p. 1552.

[39] Fagan, West, and Holland, p. 1553.

[40] Fagan, West, and Holland, p. 1554.

[41] Fagan, West, and Holland, p. 1589.

[42] Alexander, p. 92.

[43] Alexander, p. 13.

[44] Alexander, p. 3.

[45] Ooms, Herman. Tokugawa Village Practice: Class, Status, Power, Law. Berkeley: University of California Press, 1996, pp. 244-5.

[46] Alexander, p. 183.

[47] Alexander, p. 192.

[48] Alexander, p. 195.
[49] Du Bois, p. 699.
[50] Western, Dr. Bruce and Dr. Becky Pettit. Collateral Costs: Incarceration's Effect on Economic Mobility. Washington, DC: The Pew Charitable Trusts, 2010, p. 6.
[51] Myrdal, p. 556.

Chapter II

Black Poverty

But here is the challenge to our democracy: In this nation I see tens of millions of its citizens—a substantial part of its whole population—who at this very moment are denied the greater part of what the very lowest standards of today call the necessities of life ... I see millions of families trying to live on incomes so meager that the pall of family disaster hangs over them day by day ... I see millions denied education, recreation, and the opportunity to better their lot and the lot of their children ... I see one-third of a nation ill-housed, ill-clad, ill-nourished. Franklin D. Roosevelt's Second Inaugural Address.

These are exactly the conditions, 75 years after Roosevelt's great speech, in which African-Americans live today: one-third in poverty. What is even more distressing is that nearly half of African-American children grow up in households with incomes below the poverty level.[1] This is in part the effect of the historical rigidity of American income and wealth class boundaries. For example, in 1860 the wealthiest 1% of the residents of the nation's largest cities held 45% of the wealth of those cities. For much of the nineteenth century all families below the second percentile possessed less than ten dollars in assets and "there were forces at work in the American economy during the nineteenth century that tended to produce greater inequality in the distribution of wealth over time. "[2] These "forces" included those giving rise to the great concentrations of wealth seized by the men who controlled the Trusts, chiefly, the ruthless exercise of monopoly and police power. It was only during "The Great Compression" of the mid-twentieth century that inequality declined and economic mobility increased. This temporary situation was reified as "the American Dream," when that term was not limited to the aspiration of working people to own a house, a car, a refrigerator or their supposed longing for a wide choice of breakfast foods. Contrary to this Madison Avenue ideology, for much of the nation's history the America of equal opportunity and upward mobility has rarely been anything more than a dream.

The Pew Charitable Trust's 2012 report *Pursuing the American Dream: Economic Mobility Across Generations* documents what now appears to be the end of the Great Compression and with it the end of the tattered remnants of American exceptionalism. According to the report, there is now, once again, little inter-generational mobility in this country and what there is, is decreasing. The report finds that "Americans raised at the bottom and top of the family *income* ladder are likely to remain there as adults"[3] and an astonishing two-thirds of those raised at the top and bottom of the *wealth* distribution also remain in those positions as adults. America is not supposed to have these rigid multi-generational class boundaries and it is this part of the report that received the most media attention.

Less—hardly any—media attention was paid to the part of the report concerned with the issue of race. The report's authors found that "Over half of blacks (53 percent) raised in the bottom of the family income ladder remain stuck in the bottom as adults … Half of blacks (56 percent) raised in the middle of the family income ladder fall to the bottom …" As a result, more than half of Black families are at the bottom of the income ladder—half of those because they were born there, the rest because they fell down to there. The report shows that this situation is exacerbated by the fact that while 65% of Black families have incomes in the bottom fifth of the distribution, a full 83% of Black families are in the bottom two-fifths of the national income distribution. (On the other hand only 11% of White families have incomes in that bottom fifth of the distribution, and just 32% of White families can be found in the bottom two fifths.)

Few Black families can be classified as solidly middle class or higher. Only 2% of Black families make it into the highest fifth of the income scale, as compared to 23% of White families.

Analyzing income and wealth together, the Pew Charitable Trusts again found little mobility for Black Americans: "More than half of black adults (53 percent for family income and 50 percent for family wealth) raised at the bottom remain stuck there as adults, but only a third of whites (33 percent for both) do." In a technical note, the report's authors observe that there are too few Black families in the highest income and wealth quintiles to provide a basis for estimates. That is, in the income and wealth quintiles, which include nearly half of White families, the number of Black families is statistically insignificant.

The racial *percentage* distribution for family income is shown in this chart:

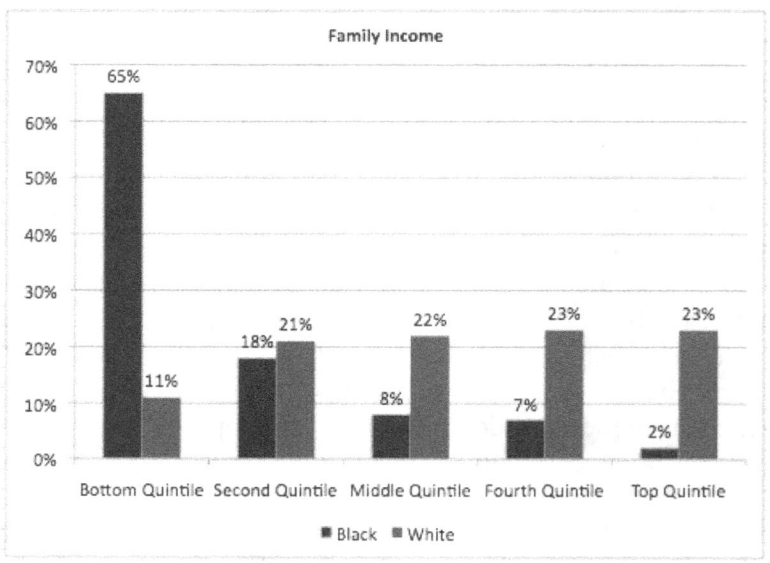

Adapted from The Pew Charitable Trust's 2012 report *Pursuing the American Dream: Economic Mobility Across Generations.*

The next chart converts these percentages to population figures:

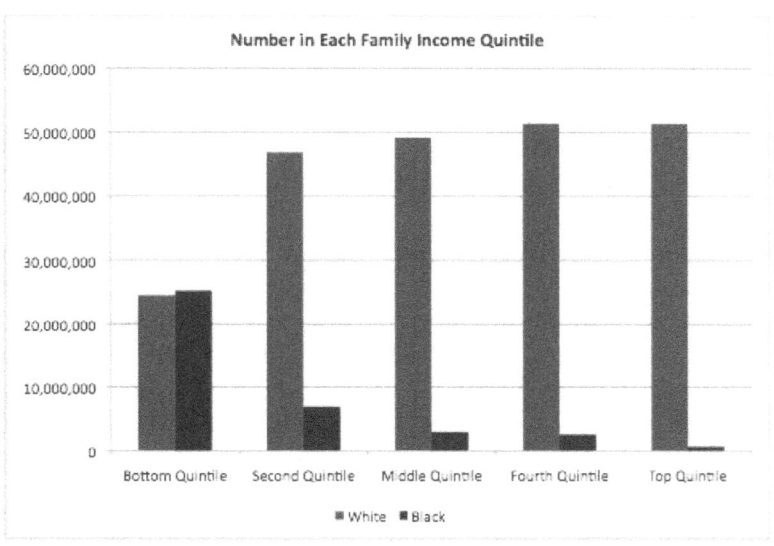

The bottom population quintile includes approximately equal numbers of Black and White Americans, while, as already observed, there are few Black Americans in the higher quintiles (7 million in the second, 3 million in the middle, 2.7 million in the fourth, 800,000 in the fifth).

Of the approximately 53 million people in the top 20% of the income distribution, at least 50 million are White and this disproportionality increases as we approach closer to the wealthiest 1% of Americans. High income Black families are "too few to report estimates." In other words, we can safely assume, as we all in fact do, that if a family has a top income, it is White, not Black. The exceptions – a few names will come to mind – simply make the case more clearly evident. No one bothers to name the White families in the 1%. We can as readily assume that if a family is Black, it is most likely poor. Moreover, perhaps two-thirds of the poorest 20% of Americans are either Black or Hispanic, groups which represent less than half that proportion of the general population.

The picture is much the same if we look at wealth rather than income. According to the Pew report: "Only 23 percent of blacks raised in the middle exceed their parents' wealth compared with 56 percent of whites. Only in the bottom quintile do a majority of blacks surpass their parents' wealth, but a black-white gap of 8 percentage points still exists."[4] (There are virtually no African-Americans born into the top two wealth quintiles, which include more than half of White, non-Hispanics.)

The Pew report tells us that class lines in America are not only becoming more marked, as is now widely recognized, but that they are becoming more rigid, with what intergenerational mobility there is increasingly dependent on educational attainment. A further analysis of the data shows that America's class divides are also increasingly race-based and that the correlation between family income and educational opportunity (or the lack thereof) is increasingly locking Black families in multi-generational poverty. An implicit message of the Pew Charitable Trusts' report is that this system of what is in effect a race-based class — or caste — structure appears to becoming permanent in the United States.

One-third of Americans living in poverty are Black — more than twice their share in the general population. However, the percentage of people living in poverty who are Black varies enormously among the states, from 4% in Utah and Maine to 62% in Mississippi (and 83% in the District of Columbia). Some of this variation, of course, has to do with the Black percentage of the population in each state, as shown in this chart:

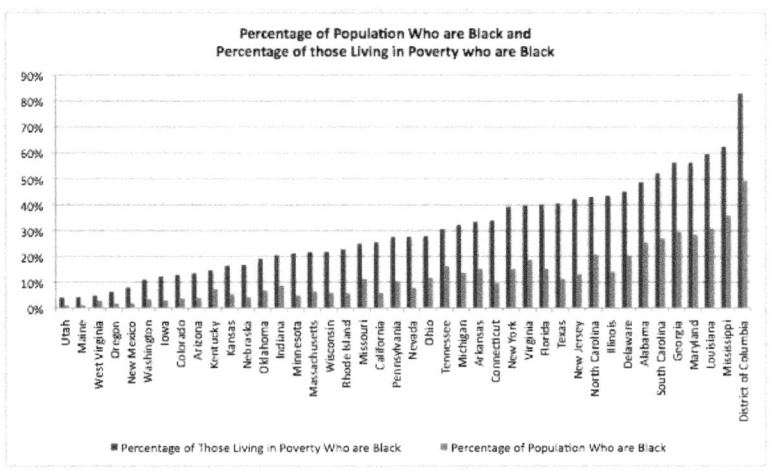

U.S. Census, The 2012 Statistical Abstract and Poverty Status in the Past 12 Months 2010. American Community Survey 1-Year Estimates.

The states where few of the poor are Black are the states where there are few African-Americans. The following chart shows the same data, sorted by the difference between the percentage of each state's population living in poverty who are Black and the percentage of the total population of the state's population who are Black.

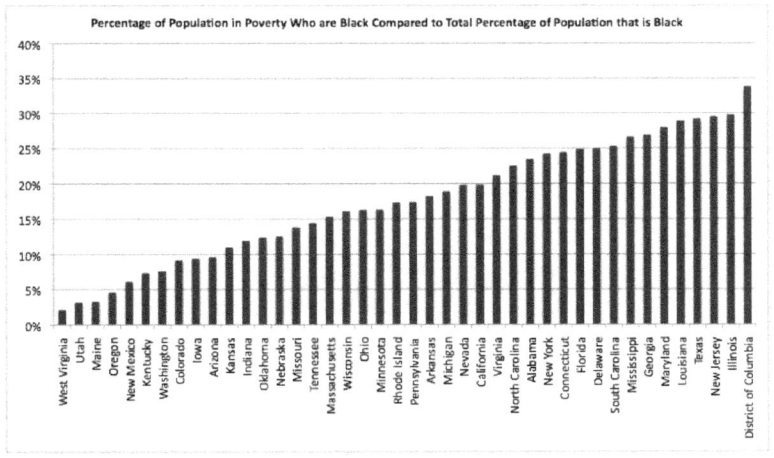

U.S. Census, The 2012 Statistical Abstract and Poverty Status in the Past 12 Months 2010. American Community Survey 1-Year Estimates.

This chart displays the disproportionality of Black poverty in each state, from West Virginia, Utah, Maine and Oregon, where the representation of African-Americans among the population that is poor in the state is only slightly above the representation of African-Americans in the general population, to Maryland, Louisiana, Texas, New Jersey, Illinois and the District of Columbia, where African-Americans are grossly over-represented among the poor. This racial disproportionality of poverty is most acute in New Jersey and Illinois (the District of Columbia is obviously a special case), but after that come eight former Jim Crow states. States where the lowest percentage of those living in poverty are Black tend to be those with few Black residents or where the White (or in New Mexico, Hispanic) population is particularly impoverished, such as West Virginia and Kentucky.

Remarkably, there is very little correlation between Black and White poverty rates *within* states. The White poverty rate in Maine is only one point above the national average; the Black poverty rates in West Virginia and Kentucky are below the national average. Only in Maryland are the poverty rates for both Black and White Americans correspondingly low in respect to those in all other states.

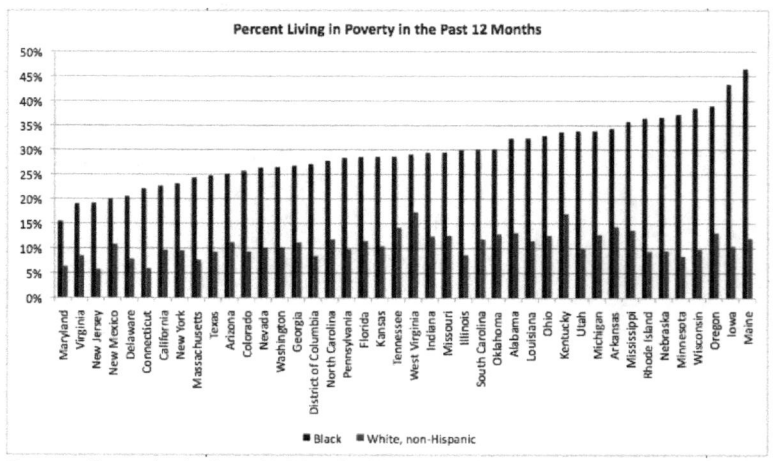

Poverty Status in the Past 12 Months 2010 American Community Survey 1-Year Estimates.

The states with the most White, non-Hispanic, people living in poverty are California, Florida, Ohio, New York, Texas and Pennsylvania. These are the six most populous states and they are evenly spread across the country's regions. Those states with the most Black people living in poverty are Florida, Georgia, Texas, New York, North Carolina and Illinois: four Southern states and two northern states with large urban populations. More Black than White people in Georgia live in poverty, despite the fact that the state has twice as many White as Black residents. This is also true of Louisiana, Mississippi, South Carolina and Maryland. All these were slave states. All had Jim Crow laws. That heritage remains.[*]

Sorting the states by the *number* of Black persons living in poverty, we find that there is a great concentration in the South and certain northern, formerly industrial states: New York, Illinois, Michigan and Ohio, as well as California. The concentration of African-Americans living in poverty who are in the core former-slave-states is an artifact of the influence of history and the continuation of the heritage of the subordinate status of African-Americans in those states. It is notable that this subordinate status, manifesting as economic immobility, now extends to the nation as a whole.

---

[*] Maryland is an economic outlier in this group: in spite of the state's comparatively low Black poverty level, its extraordinarily low White poverty level results in Black residents forming a disproportionate share of the state's poor.

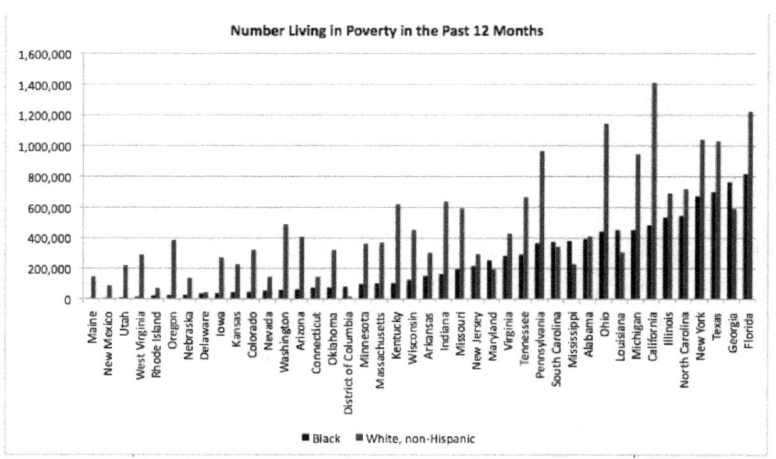

Poverty Status in the Past 12 Months 2010 American Community Survey 1-Year Estimates.

Economic inequality in the United States, today as throughout its history, is racialized. To use the Disraelian cliché, we are truly two nations, one Black and poor, kept poor, the other White, showing an income distribution much like that of a developed country. Between these is a shifting immigrant population — first German and Irish, then eastern and southern European (especially Italian), now Hispanic (overwhelmingly Mexican) — which traditionally comes into American life level with or just above the Black population and then is gradually assimilated to the White group. The great immigration from Italy (especially Southern Italy and Sicily) in the early twentieth century was an immigration of farm workers with low literacy rates in any language. They settled in cities and factory towns, in or near Black neighborhoods. Today the median family income of Italian-Americans is $78,480, considerably above the median income for all American families ($61,455) and higher still than that of Black families ($40,140). It is highly probable that this will be the path followed by the more recent immigrations from Latin America. This comparative, occasional, income mobility of immigrants often conceals, is used to conceal, the economic immobility of African-Americans.

What are the ways in which Black poverty and Black intergenerational economic immobility are maintained? One is educational inequities, to which we will turn in the next chapter. Another is the mass incarceration discussed in the previous chapter, the economic implications of which we will now consider.

It is well-known (at least since the Moynihan Report) that family structures vary by race. This data is from the 2010 Census:

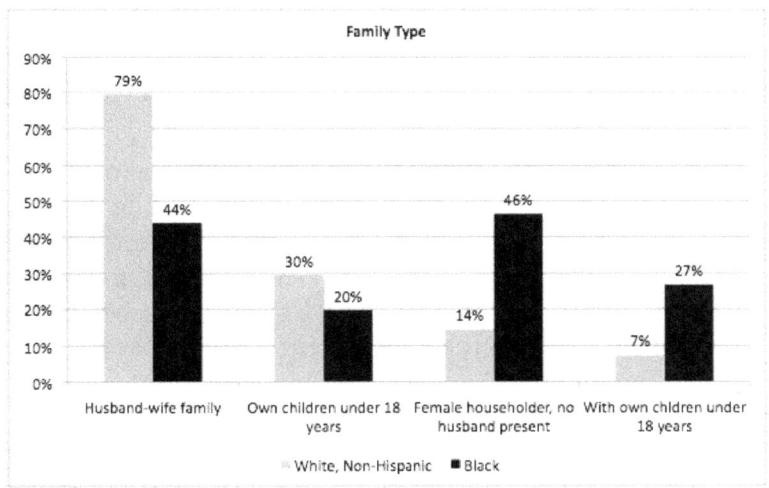

Family Type by Presence and Age of Own Children. 2010 Census Summary File 1.

Nearly 80% of White, non-Hispanic, households were traditional "Husband-wife" families. Thirty percent of those traditional White families included their "own children under 18 years." Fourteen percent of White, non-Hispanic, households were those of unmarried women and 7% were "Female householder, no husband present" with "own children under 18 years." Among Black households, less than half, 44%, were traditional "Husband-wife" families. Families of that type including their "own children under 18 years" were just 20% of all Black families. On the other hand, 46% (4.3 million), of all Black families were listed by the 2010 Census as "Female householder, no husband present" and 27% (2.5 million) were "Female householder, no husband present" with their "own children under 18 years." In other words, nearly half of Black women are at the head of their own household — three times the White rate — and it is four times more likely that a Black child will live with his mother alone than live with both parents. Of those 2.4 million African-American families, "Female householder, no husband present" with their "own children under 18 years," 1.3 million (54%) had incomes below the poverty level in 2010.[5] (The *number* of such White, non-Hispanic, households is similar, 1.5 million female household families with children under 18 years and incomes below poverty, but the *percentage* is much lower: 33% of such families.)

It is approximately equally likely that a Hispanic or White, non-Hispanic, child living in poverty will be living with both parents or with a mother alone. For the 3.5 million Black children living in poverty, it is overwhelmingly more likely that they will be the children of a woman raising her children without a husband, or any of his income, to help.

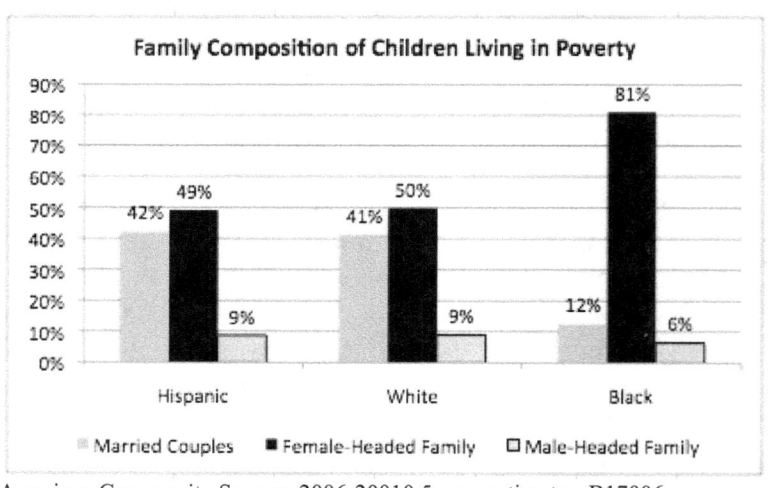

American Community Survey, 2006-20010 5-year estimates, B17006.

Those 1.3 million African-American households with children being raised by their mothers alone with incomes below the poverty line are a crucial group for public policy. Moving those families, or a substantial number of them, out of poverty will increase education achievement and decrease mass incarceration. Or, to look at it in another way, increasing educational achievement and decreasing mass incarceration would move a substantial number of those 1.3 million families out of poverty.

Lance Hannon's and Robert DeFina's study, "The Impact of Mass Incarceration on Poverty" (2009) determines that, for the nation as a whole, "had mass incarceration not occurred [during the period 1980 to 2004], poverty would have decreased by more than 20%, or about 2.8 percentage points. At the national scale, this translates into several million fewer people in poverty had mass incarceration not occurred …" They go on to note that "it is likely that the effects of mass incarceration on poverty are even greater than those presented in this analysis."[6] Given the disproportionate number and percentage of African-American men among the incarcerated, the effect on Black poverty of mass incarceration is obviously substantial. How substantial?

The overwhelming proportion of those incarcerated are men. This obvious gender disparity has implications that are perhaps less obvious, but nonetheless crucial in impoverished Black neighborhoods. Professor Western has observed that "… the main effect of the prison boom on gender relations is due precisely to the approximate fact that men go to prison, and women are left in free society to raise families and contend with ex-prisoners returning home after release."[7] Moreover, before most young men who go to prison do so, they were contributing significantly to their households' income. This contribution of future prisoners may have been enough to keep those families out of poverty.[8] Once they are incarcerated, that contribution comes to an end and in many, if not most, cases their families fall into poverty. While a man is in jail, his partner (or former partner) and her children are deprived of his income and after he is released, given the employment difficulties of ex-prisoners, they are deprived of his full potential as a worker and thus the income he can provide to his children's household is severely limited. In most cases, from the moment of arrest (if not before[9]), his children live in a household with an income below the poverty line. Hannon and DeFina find that this effect, unsurprisingly, is "especially pronounced in areas with a high proportion of non-White residents,"[10] that is, ghettoes, where most Black men of an age to have young children are likely to be incarcerated, on parole or probation. Joseph Stiglitz in his book *The Price of Inequality* cites a study by Devah Pager showing that "a white man with a criminal record is slightly more likely to be considered for a job than a black man with no criminal past. Thus, on average, being black reduces employment opportunities substantially, and more so with ex-offenders."[11]

The following chart shows the ratio between the *number* of African-Americans incarcerated in each state to the number of school-age African-American children living in poverty in that state, along with African-American incarceration *rates* per 100,000.

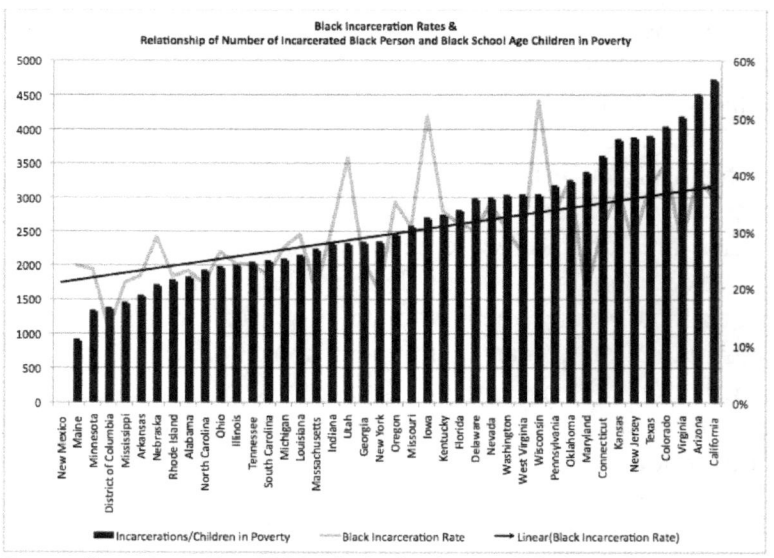

Poverty Status in the Past 12 Months by Sex by Age (Black or African-American Alone). 2010 American Community Survey 1-Year Estimates and Bureau of Justice Statistics.

The interpretation of this chart is that in Alabama, for example, there are 23,600 African-Americans who are incarcerated and 107,500 school age children with incomes below the poverty level.[†] The ratio between those numbers is 22% (right scale). The incarceration rate for African-Americans in Alabama is 1,916 per 100,000 (left scale). States with higher incarceration rates for African-Americans show a higher ratio of incarcerated African-Americans to school-age African-American children living in poverty. Or to put it as simply as possible, other things being equal, the more African-Americans a state incarcerates, the more of its African-American children live in poverty, generation after generation. Extraordinary incarceration rates of African-American men are—at a minimum—*associated with* extraordinary poverty rates for African-American children. This should seem obvious to policy makers and, for example, district attorneys.

Over half of the Black men in prison have children and nearly as many were living with those children when they were sent to prison.[12] As there are over 800,000 Black men who are incarcerated, it is reasonable to estimate that as many as one-third of the Black families living in poverty are the families of incarcerated men and many more are the families of formerly incarcerated men. According to Professor Pamela Oliver and her associates at the University of Wisconsin, "High rates of Black male imprisonment are associated ... with reduced family income, especially in less educated families ... Thus, one clear path of effect from imprisonment to child poverty is through the reduction in male incomes due to imprisonment."[13] This reduction in incomes takes place not only during the years while the father is in prison, but continues for years after his release from prison.[‡] Western and Pettit calculate that incarceration reduces earnings for Black men through age 48

[†] The overwhelming majority of prisoners are Black men. For example, just 8% of incarcerated African-Americans in Alabama are female.

[‡] The effect of post-incarceration earnings reduction for the Black community is more than four times that for the White community.

by 44%.[14] As the median income for Black males is approximately $40,000, a 44% reduction brings that income to the poverty level. Looked at in another way, from the point of view of the children themselves, Professor Pettit concludes that "... one-quarter of recent cohorts of black children can expect to have a parent imprisoned during their childhood ... Among recent cohorts of children of high school dropouts ... 62 percent of black children had a parent who went to prison before they reached age seventeen."[15]

The term "mass incarceration" does not only refer to the total number of incarcerated Black men; it also points to the concentration of incarcerations in high poverty neighborhoods. That concentration results in profoundly negative effects for those neighborhoods as well as impoverishment for the individual families of prisoners. The incarceration of young adult Black males has significant economic consequences not only for the partners (or former partners) of prisoners and ex-prisoners, not only for their own children, but also for the neighborhood and for the wider community. There is, for example, a 9% reduction in average incomes for all Black men, incarcerated or not, attributable to mass incarceration.[16] Hannon and DeFina find that concentrated mass incarceration "disrupts a neighborhood's informal mechanisms of social control and social support by, for instance, breaking up families, removing purchasing power from the neighborhood, increasing reliance on government support programs, and generally erecting even higher barriers to legitimate development and financial well-being than are currently faced. The detrimental effects of mass incarceration on a community's collective efficacy may ultimately lead to a type of 'durable inequality' where residents cannot escape what might otherwise be only episodic poverty."[17] This is a marginal effect in the White, non-Hispanic, community, more important in certain Hispanic communities, disastrous in Black communities.

Surveying this situation, Professor Western believes that if "prisons affected no one except the criminals on the inside, they would matter less.

But, after thirty years of penal population growth, the impact of America's prisons extends far beyond their walls. By zealously punishing law-breakers — including a large new class of nonviolent drug offenders — the criminal justice system at the end of the 1990s drew into its orbit families and whole communities. These most fragile families and neighborhoods were the least equipped to counter any shocks or additional deprivations."[18]

Specifically, "… the penal system has become so large that it is now an important part of a uniquely American system of social stratification."[19] The operations of the drug laws, policing and court sentencing practices criminalize a large part of the Black community — criminalize in the sense that they are designated as and treated as criminals by the representatives of the criminal justice system. We have already calculated that this results in the incarceration of approximately 100,000 young adult Black males annually for drug offenses, men who would not have been incarcerated if they had been White. We have seen that in addition, the poorer the community, of any race or ethnicity, the more violent crimes occur there. The more violent crimes, the more long-term incarcerations and as a result the poorer the community. This is not to say that violent crimes do not deserve punishment, but just that for our purposes here we can observe that the increasing impoverishment of American families in the lower tenth or lower fifth income levels accelerates this increasing rate of violent felonies, perhaps as much as do the operations of the drug laws.[20]

Mass incarceration, rooted in a history of African-American slavery and debt peonage, impoverishes Black households, concentrating the Black population in segregated communities with few employment opportunities and extensive opportunities for violence. As a result, the poverty rate for African-Americans is close to triple that for White, non-

Hispanics. This extraordinary poverty rate has direct effects on the educational opportunities and achievements of male Black children, which, in turn, affect incarceration rates and income.

Appendix to Chapter II

TABLE 3

Poverty by Race: 2010

Sorted by State

State	Black Population			White, non-Hispanic, Population			% in Poverty Black
	Total	In Poverty	% in Poverty	Total	In Poverty	% in Poverty	
AL	1,214,146	393,012	32	3,143,931	412,021	13	49
AK			-	447,762	31,176	7	0
AZ	252,549	63,436	25	3,638,511	406,995	11	13
AR	445,876	153,313	34	2,120,165	304,692	14	33
CA	2,135,645	483,682	23	14,651,142	1,410,920	10	26
CO	183,980	47,299	26	3,465,807	323,115	9	13
CT	341,051	75,389	22	2,469,867	146,727	6	34
DE	181,767	37,295	21	574,976	45,286	8	45
DC	297,061	80,412	27	192,065	16,327	9	83
FL	2,871,335	819,923	29	10,675,274	1,223,852	11	40
GA	2,865,120	766,120	27	5,299,018	592,696	11	56
HI	-	-	-	296,514	34,540	12	0
ID	-	-	-	1,297,823	175,000	13	0
IL	1,789,282	536,009	30	7,993,173	692,456	9	44
IN	559,695	164,772	29	5,141,882	639,396	12	20
IA	88,421	38,307	43	2,618,005	274,264	10	12
KS	156,018	44,588	29	2,173,356	227,387	10	16
KY	314,868	105,916	34	3,660,423	621,513	17	15
LA	1,395,184	452,213	32	2,678,996	306,831	11	60
ME	14,215	6,609	46	1,223,358	147,330	12	4
MD	1,643,825	254,627	15	3,094,191	196,951	6	56
MA	423,099	103,037	24	4,841,263	370,875	8	22
MI	1,337,073	452,978	34	7,410,353	946,254	13	32
MN	262,167	97,622	37	4,318,546	362,636	8	21
MS	1,065,499	381,680	36	1,679,572	229,229	14	62
MO	669,969	197,416	29	4,724,876	593,549	13	25

MT	-	-	-	848,046	111,798	13	0
NE	75,803	27,770	37	1,462,869	139,195	10	17
NV	210,778	55,531	26	1,440,666	145,987	10	28
NH	-	-	-	1,176,571	89,704	8	0
NJ	1,134,470	217,222	19	5,124,935	295,484	6	42
NM	38,509	7,696	20	821,457	89,078	11	8
NY	2,911,314	673,149	23	10,988,992	1,042,885	9	39
NC	1,967,127	545,359	28	6,086,981	719,769	12	43
ND	-	-	-	580,282	60,913	10	0
OH	1,346,553	443,187	33	9,128,156	1,144,398	13	28
OK	252,527	75,973	30	2,509,692	322,420	13	19
OR	66,645	25,977	39	2,956,544	387,946	13	6
PN	1,295,664	367,398	28	9,808,880	967,893	10	28
RI	58,836	21,463	36	773,566	72,570	9	23
SC	1,246,878	374,996	30	2,895,144	343,532	12	52
SD	-	-	-	669,926	69,217	10	0
TN	1,023,039	293,003	29	4,697,635	667,305	14	31
TX	2,836,244	701,992	25	11,147,574	1,034,109	9	40
UT	27,567	9,334	34	2,195,404	219,568	10	4
VT	-	-	-	567,507	69,265	12	0
VA	1,495,444	284,105	19	5,054,213	429,776	9	40
WA	227,681	60,263	26	4,806,075	490,095	10	11
WV	50,921	14,817	29	1,684,754	292,147	17	5
WI	329,333	126,899	39	4,624,503	454,373	10	22
WY	-	-	-	-	-	10	0

B17001A & B: Poverty Status in the Past 12 Months by Sex by Age (Black Or African American or White Non-Hispanic Alone).

TABLE 4

Poverty by Race: 2010

Sorted by Percent Black in Poverty

State	Black Population			White, non-Hispanic, Population			% Black in Poverty
	Total	In Poverty	% Poverty	Total	In Poverty	% Poverty	
NH	-	-	-	1,176,571	89,704	8	0
SD	-	-	-	669,926	69,217	10	0
ND	-	-	-	580,282	60,913	10	0
ME	14,215	6,609	46	1,223,358	147,330	12	4
IA	88,421	38,307	43	2,618,005	274,264	10	12
OR	66,645	25,977	39	2,956,544	387,946	13	6
WI	329,333	126,899	39	4,624,503	454,373	10	22
MN	262,167	97,622	37	4,318,546	362,636	8	21
NE	75,803	27,770	37	1,462,869	139,195	10	17
MS	1,065,499	381,680	36	1,679,572	229,229	14	62
RI	58,836	21,463	36	773,566	72,570	9	23
AR	445,876	153,313	34	2,120,165	304,692	14	33
KY	314,868	105,916	34	3,660,423	621,513	17	15
MI	1,337,073	452,978	34	7,410,353	946,254	13	32
UT	27,567	9,334	34	2,195,404	219,568	10	4
OH	1,346,553	443,187	33	9,128,156	1,144,398	13	28
AL	1,214,146	393,012	32	3,143,931	412,021	13	49
LA	1,395,184	452,213	32	2,678,996	306,831	11	60
IL	1,789,282	536,009	30	7,993,173	692,456	9	44
OK	252,527	75,973	30	2,509,692	322,420	13	19
SC	1,246,878	374,996	30	2,895,144	343,532	12	52
FL	2,871,335	819,923	29	10,675,274	1,223,852	11	40
IN	559,695	164,772	29	5,141,882	639,396	12	20
KS	156,018	44,588	29	2,173,356	227,387	10	16
MO	669,969	197,416	29	4,724,876	593,549	13	25
TN	1,023,039	293,003	29	4,697,635	667,305	14	31

WV	50,921	14,817	29	1,684,754	292,147	17	5
NC	1,967,127	545,359	28	6,086,981	719,769	12	43
PN	1,295,664	367,398	28	9,808,880	967,893	10	28
DC	297,061	80,412	27	192,065	16,327	9	83
GA	2,865,120	766,120	27	5,299,018	592,696	11	56
CO	183,980	47,299	26	3,465,807	323,115	9	13
NV	210,778	55,531	26	1,440,666	145,987	10	28
WA	227,681	60,263	26	4,806,075	490,095	10	11
AZ	252,549	63,436	25	3,638,511	406,995	11	13
TX	2,836,244	701,992	25	11,147,574	1,034,109	9	40
MA	423,099	103,037	24	4,841,263	370,875	8	22
CA	2,135,645	483,682	23	14,651,142	1,410,920	10	26
NY	2,911,314	673,149	23	10,988,992	1,042,885	9	39
CT	341,051	75,389	22	2,469,867	146,727	6	34
DE	181,767	37,295	21	574,976	45,286	8	45
NM	38,509	7,696	20	821,457	89,078	11	8
NJ	1,134,470	217,222	19	5,124,935	295,484	6	42
VA	1,495,444	284,105	19	5,054,213	429,776	9	40
MD	1,643,825	254,627	15	3,094,191	196,951	6	56
AK	-	-	-	447,762	31,176	7	0
HI	-	-	-	296,514	34,540	12	0
ID	-	-	-	1,297,823	175,000	13	0
MT	-	-	-	848,046	111,798	13	0
VT	-	-	-	567,507	69,265	12	0
WY	-	-	-	-	-	10	0

TABLE 5

Poverty by Race: 2010

Sorted by Percent in Poverty Who are Black

State	Black Population			White, non-Hispanic, Population			% in Poverty who are Black
	Total	In Poverty	% Poverty	Total	In Poverty	% Poverty	
DC	297,061	80,412	27	192,065	16,327	9	83
MS	1,065,499	381,680	36	1,679,572	229,229	14	62
LA	1,395,184	452,213	32	2,678,996	306,831	11	60
GA	2,865,120	766,120	27	5,299,018	592,696	11	56
MD	1,643,825	254,627	15	3,094,191	196,951	6	56
SC	1,246,878	374,996	30	2,895,144	343,532	12	52
AL	1,214,146	393,012	32	3,143,931	412,021	13	49
DE	181,767	37,295	21	574,976	45,286	8	45
IL	1,789,282	536,009	30	7,993,173	692,456	9	44
NC	1,967,127	545,359	28	6,086,981	719,769	12	43
NJ	1,134,470	217,222	19	5,124,935	295,484	6	42
FL	2,871,335	819,923	29	10,675,274	1,223,852	11	40
TX	2,836,244	701,992	25	11,147,574	1,034,109	9	40
VA	1,495,444	284,105	19	5,054,213	429,776	9	40
NY	2,911,314	673,149	23	10,988,992	1,042,885	9	39
CT	341,051	75,389	22	2,469,867	146,727	6	34
AR	445,876	153,313	34	2,120,165	304,692	14	33
MI	1,337,073	452,978	34	7,410,353	946,254	13	32
TN	1,023,039	293,003	29	4,697,635	667,305	14	31
OH	1,346,553	443,187	33	9,128,156	1,144,398	13	28
PN	1,295,664	367,398	28	9,808,880	967,893	10	28
NV	210,778	55,531	26	1,440,666	145,987	10	28
CA	2,135,645	483,682	23	14,651,142	1,410,920	10	26
MO	669,969	197,416	29	4,724,876	593,549	13	25
RI	58,836	21,463	36	773,566	72,570	9	23
WI	329,333	126,899	39	4,624,503	454,373	10	22

MA	423,099	103,037	24	4,841,263	370,875	8	22
MN	262,167	97,622	37	4,318,546	362,636	8	21
IN	559,695	164,772	29	5,141,882	639,396	12	20
OK	252,527	75,973	30	2,509,692	322,420	13	19
NE	75,803	27,770	37	1,462,869	139,195	10	17
KS	156,018	44,588	29	2,173,356	227,387	10	16
KY	314,868	105,916	34	3,660,423	621,513	17	15
AZ	252,549	63,436	25	3,638,511	406,995	11	13
CO	183,980	47,299	26	3,465,807	323,115	9	13
IA	88,421	38,307	43	2,618,005	274,264	10	12
WA	227,681	60,263	26	4,806,075	490,095	10	11
NM	38,509	7,696	20	821,457	89,078	11	8
OR	66,645	25,977	39	2,956,544	387,946	13	6
WV	50,921	14,817	29	1,684,754	292,147	17	5
ME	14,215	6,609	46	1,223,358	147,330	12	4
UT	27,567	9,334	34	2,195,404	219,568	10	4
ID	-	-	-	1,297,823	175,000	13	0
MT	-	-	-	848,046	111,798	13	0
HI	-	-	-	296,514	34,540	12	0
VT	-	-	-	567,507	69,265	12	0
WY	-	-	-		-	10	0
AK	-	-	-	447,762	31,176	7	0
NH	-	-	-	1,176,571	89,704	8	0
SD	-	-	-	669,926	69,217	10	0
ND	-	-	-	580,282	60,913	10	0

TABLE 6

Male Childhood Poverty: 2010

Income in the Past 12 Months Below Poverty Level

Sorted by State

State	Black Males Under 18			White Males Under 18		
	# below poverty	# above poverty	% below poverty	# below poverty	# above poverty	% below poverty
AL	78,943	95,475	45%	68,087	294,836	19%
AK	-	-	-	4,482	50,246	8%
AZ	14,077	29,312	32%	134,984	466,603	22%
AR	33,201	34,879	49%	54,858	203,383	21%
CA	85,558	187,098	31%	535,587	2,159,474	20%
CO	11,776	15,497	43%	71,510	412,599	15%
CT	14,521	35,288	29%	24,583	271,135	8%
DE	9,118	17,638	34%	8,707	54,733	14%
DC	13,978	19,378	42%	1,093	11,726	9%
FL	163,038	261,833	38%	253,228	1,120,990	18%
GA	156,473	274,544	36%	111,349	570,575	16%
HI	-	-	-	2,327	20,634	10%
ID	-	-	-	33,906	161,787	17%
IL	107,538	155,865	41%	129,117	907,319	12%
IN	35,596	51,682	41%	115,340	532,268	18%
IA	7,410	7,969	48%	40,533	275,438	13%
KS	8,041	15,183	35%	42,273	250,001	14%
KY	24,615	23,959	51%	100,130	333,329	23%
LA	98,832	114,494	46%	43,801	267,389	14%
ME	1,977	1,573	56%	21,509	104,865	17%
MD	47,854	172,263	22%	24,705	333,460	7%
MA	20,997	40,626	34%	54,017	486,503	10%
MI	94,243	98,013	49%	149,336	712,740	17%
MN	21,928	25,701	46%	50,137	460,253	10%
MS	81,093	83,372	49%	37,129	158,140	19%
MO	43,810	57,172	43%	93,772	464,011	17%
MT	-	-	-	17,342	77,709	18%
NE	6,289	6,168	50%	29,961	164,367	15%

NV	11,683	18,538	39%	45,786	177,228	21%
NH	-	-	-	11,430	118,294	9%
NJ	43,428	110,168	28%	66,959	601,066	10%
NM	1,294	3,755	26%	44,155	132,539	25%
NY	125,108	247,627	34%	191,584	1,124,177	15%
NC	111,443	168,196	40%	122,002	599,688	17%
ND	-	-	-	6,986	57,193	11%
OH	94,616	103,932	48%	194,731	864,514	18%
OK	16,614	21,312	44%	57,368	238,852	19%
OR	4,887	4,604	51%	66,656	273,946	20%
PN	66,215	120,961	35%	148,875	923,802	14%
RI	3,636	4,953	42%	10,422	72,636	13%
SC	70,890	103,951	41%	52,657	275,167	16%
SD	-	-	-	9,569	70,768	12%
TN	58,670	94,425	38%	110,854	431,889	20%
TX	138,580	290,005	32%	577,262	1,882,020	23%
UT	2,286	3,633	39%	50,606	330,068	13%
VT	-	-	-	10,007	50,025	17%
VA	52,762	147,063	26%	58,870	534,219	10%
WA	10,040	23,386	30%	90,363	481,618	16%
WV	2,293	3,507	40%	41,574	136,646	23%
WI	28,840	28,384	50%	73,232	465,340	14%
WY	-	-	-	7,006	52,347	12%

TABLE 7

Male Childhood Poverty: 2010

Sorted by Percentage Black Male Children in Poverty

State	Black Males Under 18			White Males Under 18		
	# below poverty	# above poverty	% below poverty	# below poverty	# above poverty	% below poverty
ME	1,977	1,573	56%	21,509	104,865	17%
KY	24,615	23,959	51%	100,130	333,329	23%
OR	4,887	4,604	51%	66,656	273,946	20%
NE	6,289	6,168	50%	29,961	164,367	15%
WI	28,840	28,384	50%	73,232	465,340	14%
AR	33,201	34,879	49%	54,858	203,383	21%
MI	94,243	98,013	49%	149,336	712,740	17%
MS	81,093	83,372	49%	37,129	158,140	19%
IA	7,410	7,969	48%	40,533	275,438	13%
OH	94,616	103,932	48%	194,731	864,514	18%
LA	98,832	114,494	46%	43,801	267,389	14%
MN	21,928	25,701	46%	50,137	460,253	10%
AL	78,943	95,475	45%	68,087	294,836	19%
OK	16,614	21,312	44%	57,368	238,852	19%
CO	11,776	15,497	43%	71,510	412,599	15%
MO	43,810	57,172	43%	93,772	464,011	17%
DC	13,978	19,378	42%	1,093	11,726	9%
RI	3,636	4,953	42%	10,422	72,636	13%
IL	107,538	155,865	41%	129,117	907,319	12%
IN	35,596	51,682	41%	115,340	532,268	18%
SC	70,890	103,951	41%	52,657	275,167	16%
NC	111,443	168,196	40%	122,002	599,688	17%
WV	2,293	3,507	40%	41,574	136,646	23%
NV	11,683	18,538	39%	45,786	177,228	21%
UT	2,286	3,633	39%	50,606	330,068	13%
FL	163,038	261,833	38%	253,228	1,120,990	18%
TN	58,670	94,425	38%	110,854	431,889	20%
GA	156,473	274,544	36%	111,349	570,575	16%
KS	8,041	15,183	35%	42,273	250,001	14%
PN	66,215	120,961	35%	148,875	923,802	14%

DE	9,118	17,638	34%	8,707	54,733	14%
MA	20,997	40,626	34%	54,017	486,503	10%
NY	125,108	247,627	34%	191,584	1,124,177	15%
AZ	14,077	29,312	32%	134,984	466,603	22%
TX	138,580	290,005	32%	577,262	1,882,020	23%
CA	85,558	187,098	31%	535,587	2,159,474	20%
WA	10,040	23,386	30%	90,363	481,618	16%
CT	14,521	35,288	29%	24,583	271,135	8%
NJ	43,428	110,168	28%	66,959	601,066	10%
NM	1,294	3,755	26%	44,155	132,539	25%
VA	52,762	147,063	26%	58,870	534,219	10%
MD	47,854	172,263	22%	24,705	333,460	7%
AK	-	-	-	4,482	50,246	8%
HI	-	-	-	2,327	20,634	10%
ID	-	-	-	33,906	161,787	17%
MT	-	-	-	17,342	77,709	18%
NH	-	-	-	11,430	118,294	9%
ND	-	-	-	6,986	57,193	11%
SD	-	-	-	9,569	70,768	12%
VT	-	-	-	10,007	50,025	17%
WY	-	-	-	7,006	52,347	12%

TABLE 8

Male Childhood Poverty: 2010

Sorted by Number Black Male Children in Poverty

State	Black Males Under 18			White Males Under 18		
	# below poverty level	# above poverty level	% below poverty level	# below poverty level	# above poverty level	% below poverty level
FL	163,038	261,833	38%	253,228	1,120,990	18%
GA	156,473	274,544	36%	111,349	570,575	16%
TX	138,580	290,005	32%	577,262	1,882,020	23%
NY	125,108	247,627	34%	191,584	1,124,177	15%
NC	111,443	168,196	40%	122,002	599,688	17%
IL	107,538	155,865	41%	129,117	907,319	12%
LA	98,832	114,494	46%	43,801	267,389	14%
OH	94,616	103,932	48%	194,731	864,514	18%
MI	94,243	98,013	49%	149,336	712,740	17%
CA	85,558	187,098	31%	535,587	2,159,474	20%
MS	81,093	83,372	49%	37,129	158,140	19%
AL	78,943	95,475	45%	68,087	294,836	19%
SC	70,890	103,951	41%	52,657	275,167	16%
PN	66,215	120,961	35%	148,875	923,802	14%
TN	58,670	94,425	38%	110,854	431,889	20%
VA	52,762	147,063	26%	58,870	534,219	10%
MD	47,854	172,263	22%	24,705	333,460	7%
MO	43,810	57,172	43%	93,772	464,011	17%
NJ	43,428	110,168	28%	66,959	601,066	10%
IN	35,596	51,682	41%	115,340	532,268	18%
AR	33,201	34,879	49%	54,858	203,383	21%
WI	28,840	28,384	50%	73,232	465,340	14%
KY	24,615	23,959	51%	100,130	333,329	23%
MN	21,928	25,701	46%	50,137	460,253	10%
MA	20,997	40,626	34%	54,017	486,503	10%
OK	16,614	21,312	44%	57,368	238,852	19%
CT	14,521	35,288	29%	24,583	271,135	8%
AZ	14,077	29,312	32%	134,984	466,603	22%
DC	13,978	19,378	42%	1,093	11,726	9%
CO	11,776	15,497	43%	71,510	412,599	15%

NV	11,683	18,538	39%	45,786	177,228	21%
WA	10,040	23,386	30%	90,363	481,618	16%
DE	9,118	17,638	34%	8,707	54,733	14%
KS	8,041	15,183	35%	42,273	250,001	14%
IA	7,410	7,969	48%	40,533	275,438	13%
NE	6,289	6,168	50%	29,961	164,367	15%
OR	4,887	4,604	51%	66,656	273,946	20%
RI	3,636	4,953	42%	10,422	72,636	13%
WV	2,293	3,507	40%	41,574	136,646	23%
UT	2,286	3,633	39%	50,606	330,068	13%
ME	1,977	1,573	56%	21,509	104,865	17%
NM	1,294	3,755	26%	44,155	132,539	25%
AK	-	-	-	4,482	50,246	8%
HI	-	-	-	2,327	20,634	10%
ID	-	-	-	33,906	161,787	17%
MT	-	-	-	17,342	77,709	18%
NH	-	-	-	11,430	118,294	9%
ND	-	-	-	6,986	57,193	11%
SD	-	-	-	9,569	70,768	12%
VT	-	-	-	10,007	50,025	17%
WY	-	-	-	7,006	52,347	12%

Notes

[1] "While the Census poverty rate differentiates above and below poverty at 100% of the federal poverty level (approximately $22,000 for a family of four), it is more common in education to assess poverty levels using eligibility for the federal free and reduced-price lunch (FRL) program. The threshold for this program is 185% of the federal poverty level, or approximately $41,000 for a family of four." Baker, Bruce, David Sciarra and Danielle Farrie. Is School Funding Fair? A National Report Card. Education Law Center, New Jersey. Second edition: June 2012.

[2] Gallman, Robert E. Trends in the Size Distribution of Wealth in the Nineteenth Century: Some Speculations, in Soltow, Lee, ed. Six Papers on the Size Distribution of Wealth and Income, NBER, 1969, pp. 4; 11.

[3] Emphasis added.

[4] Lopoo, Leonard and DeLeire, Thomas. Pursuing the American Dream: Economic Mobility Across Generations. Pew Charitable Trusts, 2012, p. 19.

[5] U.S. Census American Community Survey 1-Year Estimates, 2010.

[6] DeFina, Robert and Lance Hannon The Impact of Mass Incarceration on Poverty: A County-Level Analysis, 1995-2007." *The Prison Journal* 2010 90: 377 originally published online 9 September 2010 DOI: 10.1177/0032885510382085. The online version of this article can be found at: http://tpj.sagepub.com/content/90/4/377, p. 16. *Crime & Delinquency,* Crime Delinquency Online. First, published on February 12, 2009 as doi:10.1177/0011128708328864, p. 21.

[7] Western, Bruce. Punishment and Inequality in America. New York: Russell Sage Foundation, 2006, p. 15.

[8] Hannon and DeFina, p. 3.

[9] According to Defina and Hannon, "Two-thirds of people detained in jails report annual incomes under $12,000 *prior to arrest*" (emphasis added). This is half the poverty level for a family of four.

[10] DeFina, Robert H. and Lance Hannon. "The Impact of Adult Incarceration on Child Poverty: A County-Level Analysis, 1995-2007." *The Prison Journal* 2010 90: 377 originally published online 9 September 2010 DOI: 10.1177/0032885510382085. The online version of this article can be found at: http://tpj.sagepub.com/content/90/4/377, p. 16.

[11] Stiglitz, Joseph E. The Price of Inequality. London: W. W. Norton & Company, 2012, p. 69.

[12] Pettit, Becky. Invisible Men: Mass Incarceration and the Myth of Black Progress. New York: Russell Sage Foundation, 2011, p. 84.

[13] The Effect of Black Male Imprisonment on Black Child Poverty Pamela E. Oliver, Gary Sandefur, Jessica Jakubowski, and James E. Yocomp, p. 12.

[14] Western and Pettit, op.cit., p. 12.

[15] Pettit, Becky. Invisible Men: Mass Incarceration and the Myth of Black Progress. New York: Russell Sage Foundation, 2011, p. 87.

[16] Western, Dr. Bruce and Dr. Becky Pettit. Collateral Costs: Incarceration's Effect on Economic Mobility. Washington, DC: The Pew Charitable Trusts, 2010, pp. 12-4.

[17] Hannon and DeFina, p. 4.

[18] Western, Bruce. Punishment and Inequality in America. New York: Russell Sage Foundation, 2006, p. 11.

[19] Western, Punishment and Inequality in America, p. 11.

[20] Certain statistical anomalies have obscured the extent to which mass incarceration has impoverished Black communities. "The lower tail of the black wage distribution is further truncated by the joblessness of inmates. As the criminal justice system has grown, the observed wages of black men increasingly overstate the economic well-being of the general population. Moreover, reliance on estimates of the population derived from household-based samples increasingly understate racial inequality in economic outcomes." Pettit, Invisible Men, p. 53.

Chapter III

Educational Achievement of Male Black Students

The building presents a pitted and discolored concrete wall to the street. There is a fence of vertical steel bars on top of the concrete wall and coils of concertina wire atop that. Ragged black wind-blown plastic trash bags have caught in the wire. If you are allowed through the gates blocking the stairs leading up from the street, you can go around the side of the building, where there is a steel door with a lock, but no handle. There is a metal detector just inside that door. Three-quarters of the fifteen hundred students attending this school are Black. The rest are Hispanic, except for 14 White and 17 Asian children. The playing fields, such as they are, are asphalt. The corridor walls were once, perhaps, beige. They are undecorated except for the occasional memorandum of warnings and prohibitions. The district does not supply funds for science laboratories or art supplies. A third of the teachers leave each year. And so forth. A few miles away, in a White, upper middle class suburb, the school ... but you know what that school looks like, how well-equipped it is, how well-educated and dedicated its teachers are; its wide lawns and friendly trees.

Our contemporary inequities in education can be traced back to the very beginnings of public education in this country, particularly in the South. W. E. B. Du Bois found that before the Civil War, "In all Southern states (except a few of the Border states and the District of Columbia) it was forbidden to teach slaves how to read and write, and several states extended the prohibition to free Negroes."[1] He estimated that at the time of emancipation "illiteracy among the colored population was well over 95% ... which meant that less than 150,000 of the four million slaves emancipated could read and write."[2] During Reconstruction there was a great flowering of education for

African-Americans. Abolitionists, victorious, moved south, building and running schools. Former slaves who had become literate became literacy teachers. In the absence of public schools of any kind, "Between 1865 (June 1st) and September 1, 1870, the [Freedmen's] Bureau spent on education a sum which represented about one-half of the expenses of the schools. The rest was met by benevolent associations and the freedmen themselves. For some years after 1865, the education of the Negro was well-nigh monopolized by the Freedmen's Bureau, and the missions sustained by the Northern churches and organizations allied with tem. Schools of all grades, from kindergarten to the college, were established in each state."[3]

Curiously enough, for White children as well, the "public school systems, in most Southern states, began with the enfranchisement of the Negro." In South Carolina, for example, the Reconstruction constitution of 1868 for the first time obligated the state government to establish a system of universal education.[4] Similar provisions were incorporated into the Reconstruction-era constitutions of the other former Confederate states. For both White and Black students, "It is fair to say that the Negro carpetbag governments established the public schools of the South ..."[5] The history of education for African-Americans in the South after the Civil War went from individual schools under military or missionary sponsorship, to state systems put in place under the new constitutions, to — unfortunately, as it turned out — districts under local control. For Du Bois, "Local control meant the control of property and racial particularism. It stood for reaction and prejudice; and wherever there was retrogression, particularly in Negro schools, it can be traced to the increased power of the [White] county and district administrators."[6]

During the period of Jim Crow, paralleling the imposition of debt peonage, there was a systematic limitation of educational opportunities for African-Americans in the South. Once African-Americans were disenfranchised, laws were passed so as to ensure that schooling in the South for Black students was funded at much lower levels than that for White students, when not discouraged altogether. (Today, as we will see, similar inequities in funding are maintained in practice if not in law.) Myrdal commented on this point that "The interest of educating the Negroes to become faithful helots has been obvious, but the Southern whites have not even attempted to make it effective in practice. Instead, they have merely kept Negro education poor and bad."[7] (This is, perhaps, one of the few examples of irony in Myrdal's massive report.) Myrdal shows that the control of education can be, has been, and by extension now is, maintained by White politicians, even when the operations of the system appear to be in the hands of African-American professionals:

> In the main ... the control over Negro education has been preserved by other whites representing the political power of the region. [Although the] salaried officers of the movement — the college presidents, the school principals, the professors, and the teachers — are now practically all Negroes ... With this set-up, it is natural and, indeed, necessary that the Negro school adhere rather closely to the accommodating pattern ... Negro teachers on all levels are dependent on the white community leaders . . .[8]

Or as Du Bois put it: "The schools were separate but the colored schools were controlled by white officials who decided how much or rather how little should be spent upon them; who decided what could be taught and what textbooks used and the sort of subservient teachers they wanted."[9] He quotes a White official advising that when choosing between two teachers for a Black school, those (White officials) responsible should choose the less effective.

This is the background against which the lack of educational achievement by male Black students since the end of legal segregation must be considered. That comparative lack of achievement has often been attributed to the structure of the Black family. This theory is, in itself, a way to maintain the status quo. If Black students do not do well in school and they live in a family at the head of which is what the Census calls a "female householder without husband present," particularly if this "householder" has an income below the poverty level, as they often do, why inquire further? But if we do inquire further, we can rule out the family structure argument easily enough, for example by a comparison of educational outcomes for Black and Hispanic students. Most of the socio-cultural variables, except poverty itself, have different values in the Black and Hispanic communities. The Moynihan Black family consists of a woman supporting one or two children without a husband. The "typical" Hispanic household consists of a married couple with two or three children. On the other hand, Black and Hispanic families have incomes at similar points in the economic distribution and, crucially, often live in the same or neighboring communities. Their children attend the same or similar schools. It is instructive, then, to look at high school graduation rates for Black and Hispanic students, by state, sorted from highest to lowest by Hispanic graduation rates. The trends are remarkably similar:

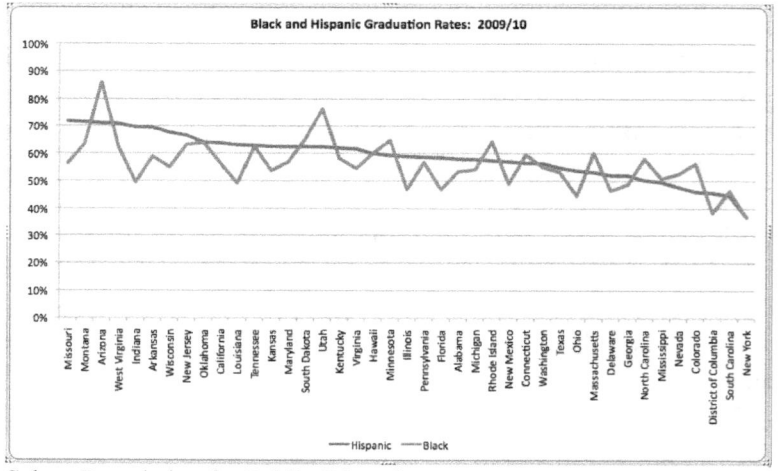

Schott Foundation for Public Education.

States with relatively high graduation rates for Hispanic students, such as New Jersey, also tend to have relatively high graduation rates for Black students; those with relatively low graduation rates for Hispanic students, such as New York, also have relatively low graduation rates for Black students. The structures of the Black and Hispanic families are unlikely to differ from one side of the Hudson River to the other, from Harlem to Newark. The similar educational outcomes for Black and Hispanic students point to something other than cultural factors in the Black family and community as the primary engine for the failure of schools to properly educate many male Black students. They point to the schools.

Three-quarters of a century ago Oliver C. Cox pointed out that after Reconstruction "… the training advocated for … the children of the poor, was intended to keep them within the occupational level of their parents; and intellectual pursuits were ruled out."[10] The schools Black children are allowed to attend today are similarly limited and, by and large, similarly segregated, which facilitates inequities in resource allocation. You only need walk through a school, such as that described at the beginning of this chapter to realize that its intellectual and cultural poverty parallels the economic poverty of the neighborhood: no student art on the walls, no laboratory benches in the science rooms, few books in the library, few — if any — computers anywhere; no music, no challenging classes. No opportunity to learn.

Researchers at The Civil Rights Project at UCLA have documented that most Black children attend schools segregated both by race/ethnicity and income.[11] While the degree of segregation declined from the 1960s (the end of *de jure* segregation in the South) to the 1980s, it has increased since then. In the 1980s, 63% of Black students attended schools with enrollments that were half or more minority, in the 2009-10 school year that percentage had risen to 74%. By 2009-10 there were six million Black students in schools that were half or more minority; three million in schools 90% to 100% minority and 1.2 million in schools that were 99-100% minority. If the last of these groupings were a single school district, it would edge out New York City's as the largest in the country.

As a matter of fact, much of New York City's public school district already looks as if it were that segregated system. The

Civil Right Project has disaggregated segregation data for each state by the intensity of segregation in each. It is striking that across all such measures, the states of New York and Illinois are among the most segregated: ranking first and second, for example, among states where the typical Black student is least likely to be in a school with White students and also for schools with more than 90% minority enrollments. These data reflect the intensity of segregation in New York City and Chicago, the nation's two largest school districts.

Table 18: *Most Segregated States for Black Students, 2009-2010*

Rank	% in 50-100% Minority Schools		Rank	% in 90-100% Minority Schools		Rank	% in 99-100% Minority Schools		Rank	% White in School of Typical Black	
1	California	90.5%	1	New York	63.6%	1	Illinois	41.4%	1	New York	17.7%
2	New Mexico	86.2%	2	Illinois	62.1%	2	Michigan	34.1%	2	Illinois	18.8%
3	New York	85.4%	3	Michigan	53.3%	3	New Jersey	26.1%	3	California	18.9%
4	Illinois	83.6%	4	Maryland	51.1%	4	Tennessee	25.9%	4	Maryland	22.0%
5	Texas	82.4%	5	New Jersey	47.6%	5	New York	23.6%	5	New Jersey	24.5%
6	Maryland	82.4%	6	Mississippi	47.5%	6	Alabama	23.4%	6	Texas	24.6%
7	Hawaii	79.1%	7	Pennsylvania	44.9%	7	Pennsylvania	23.2%	7	Mississippi	25.4%
8	Georgia	79.1%	8	Tennessee	44.1%	8	Maryland	22.9%	8	Georgia	25.5%
9	Mississippi	78.2%	9	Alabama	43.5%	9	Mississippi	20.4%	9	Michigan	26.3%
10	Nevada	78.0%	10	Wisconsin	41.4%	10	Georgia	17.4%	10	Louisiana	29.0%
11	New Jersey	77.7%	11	Georgia	40.6%	11	Missouri	13.6%	11	Tennessee	29.0%
12	Connecticut	75.9%	12	California	40.6%	12	Louisiana	12.4%	12	Alabama	29.9%
13	Florida	74.2%	13	Missouri	39.8%	13	Texas	11.9%	13	Florida	30.1%
14	Louisiana	73.9%	14	Texas	39.6%	14	Ohio	11.4%	14	Pennsylvania	30.7%
15	Michigan	73.7%	15	Ohio	36.5%	15	California	11.3%	15	Connecticut	31.4%
16	Tennessee	72.9%	16	Louisiana	36.4%	16	Indiana	10.5%	16	Nevada	31.6%
17	Pennsylvania	70.5%	17	Florida	32.9%	17	Florida	9.7%	17	Ohio	32.3%
18	Arkansas	70.1%	18	Indiana	29.6%	18	Delaware	7.3%	18	Wisconsin	33.0%
19	Ohio	69.8%	19	Connecticut	28.6%	19	Connecticut	5.4%	19	Arkansas	34.3%
20	Alabama	69.2%	20	Arkansas	25.6%	20	Arkansas	4.7%	20	Missouri	34.4%

Note: In District of Columbia, 99.1%, 90.4%, and 80.4% of black students attended a 50-100%, 90-100%, and 99-100% minority school, respectively; and only 3.3% of the student body for a typical black student was white.
Source: U.S. Department of Education, National Center for Education Statistics, Common Core of Data (CCD), Public Elementary/Secondary School Universe Survey Data

It is not an accident or happenstance that New York produces the smallest percentage of male Black high school graduates of any state. What other result could be expected from the way in which its school systems are structured? Not only are they segregated both by race and income, but their schools are funded inequitably: those schools serving low poverty neighborhoods are given more resources than those serving high poverty neighborhoods. This is the well-known Reverse Robin Hood policy of many districts and states.

The segregation of Black students would not necessarily lead to a lack of educational achievement. Many middle class African Americans of a certain age can point to elite segregated high schools that emphasized and produced high achieving students: the Talented Tenth. But today segregation is strongly linked to the lack of student achievement. Reading is the essential skill for education and by grade 8 schools and school systems have had time to provide that basic skill to their students. Grade 8 reading proficiency is, therefore, a good indicator of school and school system quality. Data from the U.S. Department of Education's National Assessment of Educational Progress (NAEP — "The Nation's Report Card") shows that as the percentage of White students in a school falls, the percentage of male Black students scoring at or above Proficient on the indicator Grade 8 Reading test falls as well: from 17% for male Black students in schools with few Black students to less than half that — 8% — for male Black students in schools that are 49% or less White.

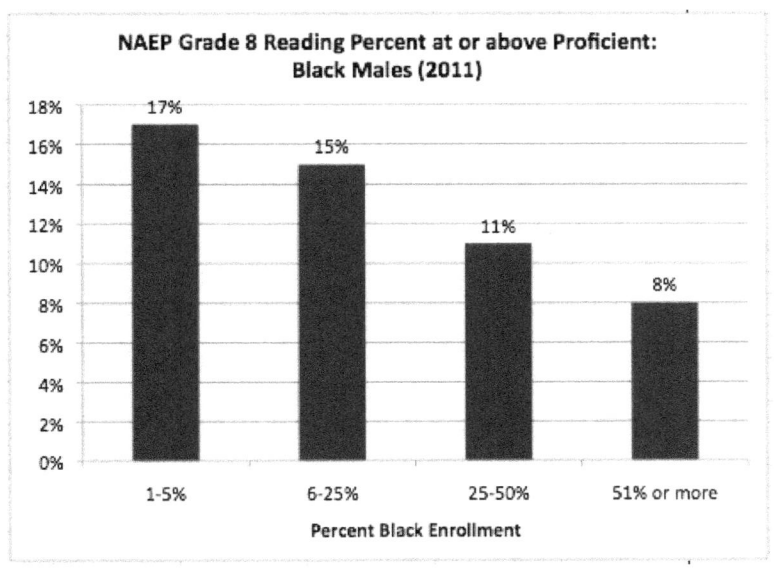

We can estimate that in 2009-2010 three-quarters of the nation's eight million Black students were in those school districts where just 8% of the Black male students scored at or above Proficient (that is, at grade level) in Grade 8 Reading. Given that the achievement levels of White students in these schools runs in parallel with that for Black students, it seems that the variable driving these effects is not the race or the home life of the students, but the quality of segregated schools: the more segregated (i.e., the fewer White students), the more inadequate, the more inadequately resourced, the school.[*]

At the time of Myrdal's study, in both the South and the North, segregation was a crucial factor in determining the quality of education on offer to African-American children. According to Myrdal: "In the North the official opinion among whites is that segregation is not compatible with equality, but ... much segregation is actually in effect as a consequence of residential segregation and of gerrymandering districts and granting permits to transfer ... In the South ... [s]egregation is usually not motivated by financial reasons but as a precaution against social equality."[12] Interestingly, according to Du Bois, during Reconstruction and immediately after:

> In nearly every state, the question of mixed and separate schools was a matter of much debate and strong feeling. There was no doubt that the Negroes in general wanted mixed schools. They wanted the advantages of contact with white children, and they wanted to have this evidence and proof of their equality.[13]

They wanted, they want, equal educational opportunity and the most direct route to this goal appears to be through integrated schools, as the prospects for schools attended exclusively by Black students receiving the resources necessary for an equal opportunity to learn seemed — seem — slight.

The national reluctance to achieve racially integrated schools has focused attention on the alternative of the economic integration of schools. However, income segregation, like racial segregation, affects basic skills proficiency. Title I of the Elementary and Secondary Education Act (1965) and its successors direct supplementary federal funding to schools and school districts in which at least 40% of the students are from low-income families. The Civil Rights

---

[*] The percentage at or above Proficient for male White students, falls from 36% at schools with half or more of their enrollment White to 17% when there are 5% or fewer White students in a school.

Project calculates that while 64% of Black students are in schools with students from low-income families—usually themselves or other Black students, only about one-third of White, non-Hispanic, students are in schools with low-income students. The results are predictable:

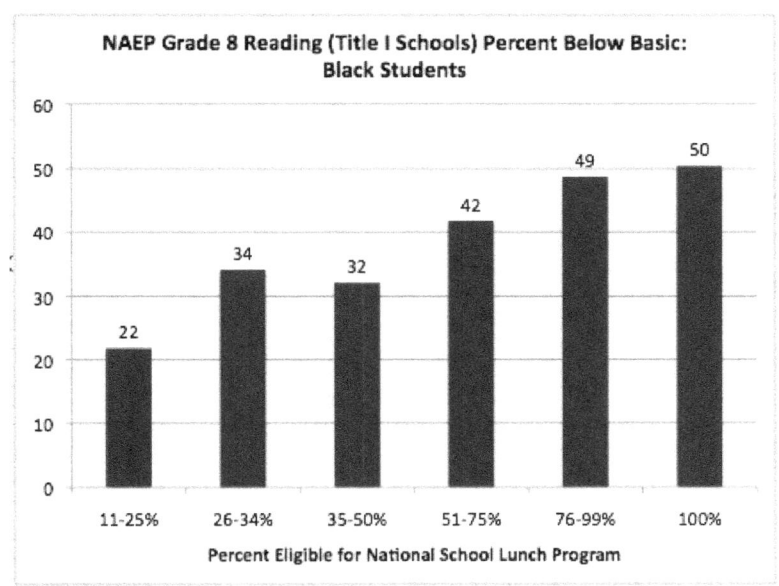

NAEP Grade 8 Reading (Title I Schools) Percent Below Basic: Black Students

As the percentage of students from families with low-incomes in these schools increases, the percentage of Black students scoring below grade level also increases. Less than a quarter of the Black students in low poverty schools score below Basic; half those in high poverty schools score below Basic on the Grade 8 Reading assessment.

Is this primarily a matter of neighborhood incomes or of individual family incomes? It is increasingly argued that we must first overcome poverty before improving educational outcomes: an argument sometimes meant to present the situation as insolvable. Others making that argument, as, for example, David Berliner, do so out of a sincere desire to change the situation.[14] Surely it is better for children if their family income is above the poverty level: better for their health, emotional well-being, nutrition and educational opportunities. But the association of the last of these, educational opportunity, with family income, is not independent of other factors. Indeed, perhaps counter-intuitively, it often has little to do directly with family income.

The predominate influence of neighborhood economic status, as opposed to an individual family's economic status, can be shown by calculating the percentage of students below Basic on NAEP's Grade 8 Reading assessment by whether or not they are eligible for the National Lunch Program themselves, on the one hand, and on the other hand by the percentage of such students enrolled in the school. The first measures the effect of family economic status; the second that of neighborhood economic status and hence, all too often, the resources provided to the school.

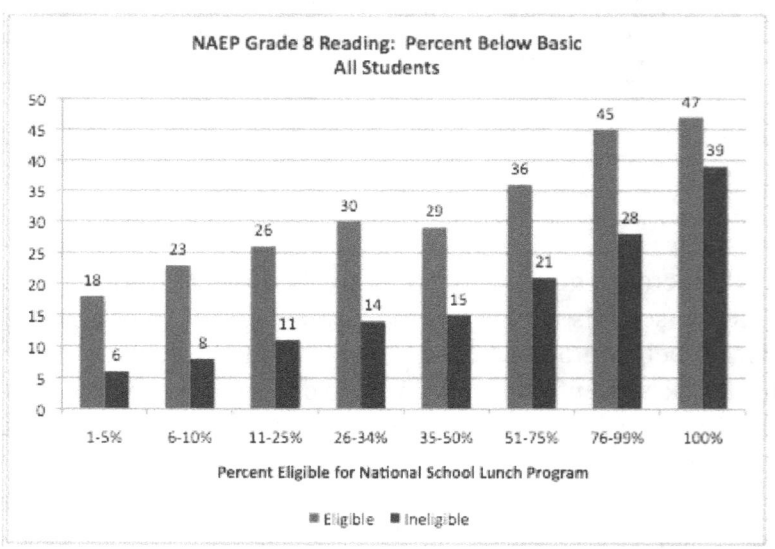

The chart shows the relative influence of individual student family economic status as compared to that of the average economic status of all students in the school. As the percentage of students living in poverty attending a school increases from 1-5% to 100%, so the percentage of students both eligible (i.e., poor, red) and ineligible (higher income, blue) who score

90

below Basic also increases. It is telling that the percentages for low-income and higher income students converge: beginning at 18% and 6%, respectively in very low poverty schools and ending at 47% and 39% in very high poverty schools. The percentage of children living in poverty attending very low poverty schools scoring below Basic is the same as or higher than that of children from higher income families attending high poverty schools, schools where a majority of the children in the school are eligible for the National Lunch Program. The average economic status of students in a school is more important than the economic status of a particular student's family. Schools in which most of the students are from families with low-incomes, and especially those in which most of the students are Black and are also from families with low-incomes, do not educate any children well. And most Black children, being from families with low-incomes, are consigned to such schools.

As a consequence of dual racial and economic segregation and the effect of these for educational opportunities, just ten percent of male Black students score at or above "proficient" (that is, at or above grade level) on the NAEP Grade 8 Reading assessment. In other words, 90% of male Black students are not proficient readers by grade 8. But that is a national average. It is significant that Black educational achievement varies by state. When analyzed on a state-by-state basis, in general, the percentage of male Black students reaching proficiency in the states parallels that for male White, non-Hispanic, students. That is, the higher the proficiency rate for male White, non-Hispanic students, the higher that for male Black students (or, perhaps, visa versa). It could be inferred from this, again, that a key variable is the overall quality of a state's school systems (not, to reiterate, some mysterious function of "the" Black family). For male Black students the range among states is from 4% Proficient or Above in California with its barely functioning urban and rural school systems to 19% in Connecticut; that is, from less than half the national average to nearly twice the national average. If all the Black students in the country attended schools where they did as well as all Black students do in Connecticut, the national achievement level for Black students would be five times what it is at present.

On the other hand, the range for male White, non-Hispanic, students is from 19% in West Virginia to 48% in Connecticut. In other words, male White, non-Hispanic, students in the lowest scoring state are taught to read as well as male Black students in the highest scoring state. Connecticut can educate its male Black students as well as West Virginia can educate its male White, non-Hispanic, students, but educates less than half the proportion of its male Black students as well as it educates its male White, non-Hispanic, students.

Why?

One answer, as we have seen, is that Black students do not attend the same schools as White students. Dual racial and economic segregation confine many of Connecticut's Black students to the failing schools of Hartford and Bridgeport, while White students—those Connecticut White students who do attend public schools—are educated in the excellent schools of the Connecticut suburbs. Black students who move a few hundred yards across a district boundary from Hartford dramatically increase their chances of graduating from high school. This is such a well-known state of affairs that a kind of educational vigilantism has arisen: White residents patrolling school parking lots to ensure that no undeserving Black or low-income children are smuggled into their schools.

Why are the schools attended by students living in poverty less adequate than those attended by students from financially better-off families? According to Berliner,

> The schools that [students living in poverty] attend are … funded differently than the schools attended by students of wealthier parents. The political power of a neighborhood and local property tax rates have allowed for apartheid-lite systems of schooling to develop in our country. For

example, 48% of high poverty schools receive less money in their local school districts than do low poverty schools ... Logic would suggest that the needs in the high poverty schools were greater, but the extant data show that almost half of the high poverty schools were receiving less money than schools in the same district enrolling families exhibiting less family poverty. [15]

Schools serving low-income families have fewer resources, and therefore less favorable outcomes, than those serving higher-income families. This intensifies the barriers to educational opportunity presented by the lack of discretionary income to spend on out-of-school education (including tutoring) and comparatively low levels of parental educational attainment. Good schools can overcome those barriers; inadequate schools are inadequate for all students, without regard to parental income and educational attainment.

Beyond these fiscal-structural issues, Dr. John H. Jackson, President of the Schott Foundation for Public Education, has focused attention on the way that Black students, especially male Black students, are "locked out" of extra resources available to White, non-Hispanic, students and "pushed out" of school itself. They are, for example, "locked out" of the extra resources of Gifted and Talented programs. The U. S. Department of Education's Office for Civil Rights (OCR) district-level data shows that the ratio of male Black to male White, non-Hispanic, students in Gifted and Talented programs ranges from 1-to-9 in Memphis and Nashville down to 1-to-1 in Montgomery County (MD) and Milwaukee.[*] That is, while Black students in Montgomery County and Milwaukee have an equal chance of receiving the increased resources characteristic of Gifted and Talented programs as White, non-Hispanic, students, they have barely more than one-tenth that opportunity in Memphis and Nashville. Are Black students nine times smarter in Milwaukee than in Nashville? Are White students one-ninth as talented in high-achieving Montgomery County as

---

[*] OCR data from New York City is incomplete and/or inaccurate.

in Memphis? In some places access to Gifted and Talented Programs varies from one neighborhood to the next. In New York City, for example, the testing of students for those programs (performed around age 4!) is intensive in the city's middle and upper class neighborhoods, and virtually non-existent in the city's poorest — and Blackest — neighborhoods. It can therefore be pointed out that participation in the city's Gifted and Talented programs is much lower for Black students than others — with the implication that this may have to do with innate ability rather than with the lack of opportunity to participate in the programs.

Another set of additional resources is associated with Advanced Placement classes. Male Black students are assigned to Advanced Placement Mathematics at less than a tenth the rate as male White, non-Hispanic students in two Louisiana districts, while they are assigned to Advanced Placement Mathematics at approximately the same rate as male White, non-Hispanic, students in the predominately Black districts of Newark, Atlanta and Cleveland. Disparities in access to Advanced Placement courses are traceable to district policy decisions, as the College Board has repeatedly advocated an "open admissions" policy for its Advanced Placement program. This policy of locking out Black students from educational opportunities — Advanced Placement and Gifted and Talented programs, among others — can be changed any afternoon. The key is in the hands of district administrators. They just have to use it.

Black students are "pushed out" by means of expulsions and out-of-school suspensions. In elementary and secondary school, out-of-school suspensions are a sensitive predicator of a student's future failure to complete high school with a regular diploma. One authoritative study found that students punished with out-of-school suspensions were three times as likely not to finish high school as those students who were not suspended.[16] According to the most recently available national survey by the U.S. Department of Education (2006), an extraordinary 19% of all male Black students were suspended from school that year, as compared with the closely aligned Hispanic and non-Hispanic White male rates of much less than half that. Out-of-school suspension ratios at the district level vary from approximately 8-to-1 in Newark and Atlanta (and 6-to-1 in two other Atlanta metropolitan area districts) down to less than twice the percentage of male Black as compared to male White, non-Hispanic, students given these punishments in districts like Boston. Are male Black students four times as well-behaved in Boston as in Atlanta?

These racial disparities in the application of school discipline policies are visible early on. Walter Gilliam of Yale University has established that in many cases prekindergarten suspension and expulsion rates for male Black children are extremely high and not wholly attributable to the behavior of those children. They are, in large part, he finds, an artifact of the attitudes and expectations of the teachers of those three- and four-year-old children, a finding confirmed by the fact that professional development for these teachers significantly lowers suspension and expulsion rates for their male Black students.[17]

At this point we can refer to a set of data similar to that for drug abuse arrests and incarcerations and even more definitively pointing to public policy and practices as the driver for these effects. The Justice Center of the Council of State Governments and the Public Policy Research Institute have published a study entitled "Breaking School Rules: A Statewide Study of How School Discipline Relates to Students' Success and Juvenile Justice Involvement."[18] The state in question is Texas and the study traces school careers for all public school students in that state who were in seventh-grade in 2000, 2001, and 2002. It was found that 83% percent of male Black students had at least one *discretionary* violation during their secondary school career (compared to 59% for non-Hispanic White students), but *mandatory* disciplinary actions were invoked at similar rates for Black and White students. The difference between discretionary and mandatory actions, in the study's vocabulary, is that the latter are based on regulated procedures and policies, set by the state, while the former are based on locally determined procedures and policies which, in general, have few if any safeguards against arbitrariness. In other words, the Texas study documented a natural experiment similar to that of drug abuse arrests: given more or less equal propensities to come afoul of objective rules ("mandatory actions"), public secondary school teachers and administrators use their discretion at the school level to punish Black students nearly a third more often than both Hispanic and White, non-Hispanic, students, and male Black students much more often yet.

The consequences for the educations of Black students in Texas are severe. According to the study: "A student who was suspended or expelled for a discretionary violation was twice as likely to repeat his or her grade compared to a student with the same characteristics, attending a similar school, who had not been suspended or expelled" (p. xi). Further, "a student who was suspended or expelled for a discretionary violation was nearly three times as likely to be in contact with the juvenile justice system the following year," and so into the criminal justice system later.[†] (Note that these are the consequences, in the main, of "discretionary," that is, unregulated, actions by local school personnel.)

[†] In Meridian, Mississippi, this process is shortened: school discipline procedures include handing Black students over to the local police: "Federal civil rights lawyers filed suit Wednesday against Meridian, Mississippi, and other defendants for operating what the government calls a school-to-prison in which students are denied basic constitutional rights, sent to court and incarcerated for minor school infractions ... The lawsuit says children who talk back to teachers, violate dress codes and commit other minor infractions are handcuffed and sent to a youth court where they are denied their rights (CNN, October 26, 2012).

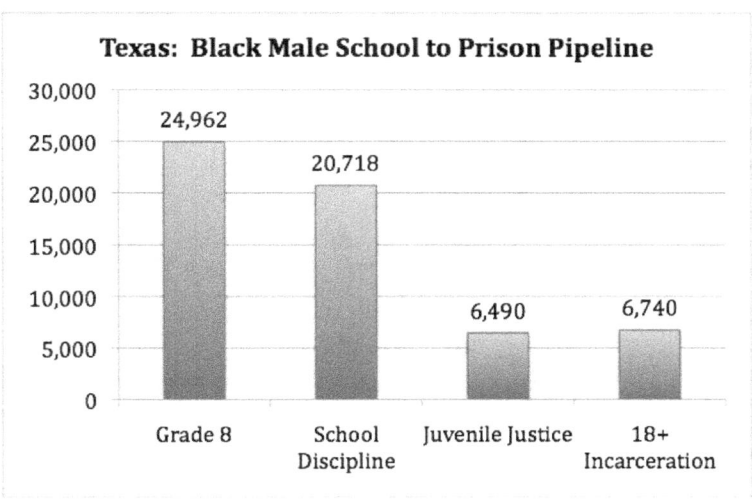

Of Texas male Black students suspended on the basis of these decisions by local school personnel, more than one-third of the cohort came into contact with the state's juvenile justice system, only a slightly lower number than the number of male Black adults incarcerated in Texas. Being "known to the police" increases the chances that a person will be arrested. It is always easier to round up the usual suspects. That is why they are the usual suspects.

Given the Texas data indicating that Black students in that state are punished at the school level with discretionary out-of-school suspensions more often than other students, we can estimate the number of male Black students punished with out-of-school suspensions in the country as a whole, who most likely would not have been if they had been Hispanic or White, non-Hispanic, and had engaged in the same behaviors. The national percentages for out-of-school suspensions were 19% for Black males, 7% for White, non-Hispanic, males and 9% for Hispanic males. Projecting on the basis of the national Hispanic numbers (because of the similarity of family economic status) would give us a figure of 400,000 excess Black male suspensions each year in the United States. Working from the Texas data, there is an excess of 250,000.

Between the two, a conservative estimate would be 300,000 Black male students punished with out-of-school suspensions each year, who would not have been removed from the classroom if they had been from any racial or ethnic background other than Black. Assuming that most suspensions are in secondary school, and counting six years of secondary school with a 7% chance of being suspended each year, it is likely that on a national basis Black male students have more than a 40% chance of out-of-school suspension for racial reasons during their secondary school careers. This happens to be approximately the percentage of young adult Black males without high school diplomas who might expect to experience incarceration as young adults.

This push-out of Black students could be ended by school district administrators any afternoon they chose to do so. Doing so might well increase the number of Black men with high school diplomas by a quarter of a million or more *each year.*

There is a high school graduation rate gender gap across all racial and ethnic groups. That for White, non-Hispanic, students is 3%. However, that for Black students is 12%: four times as great.

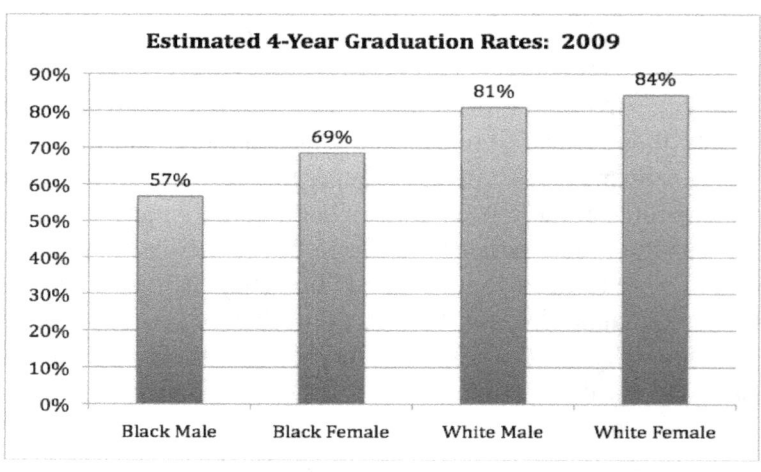

No doubt many factors contribute to this startling difference. One is likely to be racially motivated out-of-school suspensions, which primarily affect male Black students. As with mass incarceration, debt peonage, lynching and the daily cruelty of slavery itself, Black males, in particular, are made to suffer from school discipline inequities. It is not, everywhere, as it is in Meriden, Mississippi, part of an overt system of preparing male Black students for incarceration. In many places, such as in Connecticut's preschools, it is simply a reflex: Black males, even three or four year old Black males, are seen by those with authority over them as requiring disciplinary action more frequently than other males or any females. Another factor is the effect of parental incarceration, in particular the incarceration of fathers, which is especially devastating to young Black males. For the cohort due to graduate from high school in June 2010, average Black male k-8 enrollment was 300,000, but by grade 12, in the 2009-2010 school year, it had declined to approximately 250,000. Approximately 65,000 Black male students in this cohort did not graduate from high school in June, 2010. If present trends continue, 24,000 of those will be incarcerated as young men. Much of this is attributable to the effects of parental incarceration, family poverty and the quality – or lack of it – of schools in communities of concentrated poverty.

The national public high school graduation rate (grade 9 to diploma) for male Black students is 52%.[19] This is a significant increase in a decade from the rate of 41% for the 2001/2 school-year (but far lower than the 75% rate to be inferred from the Census). The graduation rate for male White, non-Hispanic, students, on the same basis, has also increased, from 70% to 78% over that period (versus the implied 85% Census rate). The gap between these Black and White, non-Hispanic, graduation rates has therefore narrowed from 29 percentage points to 26. At this pace, if nothing is done, it will take the better part of a century to close the gap between male Black and White, non-Hispanic, high school graduation rates.

Three states have achieved higher male Black than male White, non-Hispanic, graduation rates: Maine, Arizona and Vermont. Four more (Utah, Idaho, Oregon and Alaska) currently have higher male Black graduation rates than the national male White, non-Hispanic, graduation rate in the 2001/2 school year. None of these states include districts with 10,000 or more male Black students, most (except Arizona) have very few Black students. This relationship between relatively high male Black graduation rates and relatively low concentrations of Black students is supportive of the idea that integrated school systems better serve Black students than segregated systems, perhaps, as has been argued here, because schools oriented toward the education of White, non-Hispanic, students are likely to provide teachers and facilities superior to those to which majorities of Black students are consigned.[20]

If we look at the states having at least one school district enrolling 10,000 or more male Black students, that with the highest graduation rate for male Black students is New Jersey, with a graduation rate for male Black students of 63% (as compared to 90% for its male, White, non-Hispanic students). New Jersey's graduation rates for students from all racial/ethnic groups are among the best and many of the state's Black students attend integrated schools in this highly suburbanized state. These positive effects were reinforced by the "Abbott" case, which directed enhanced resources to Newark and other districts with concentrated Black and impoverished populations.[21] Of the seven states enrolling more that 200,000 male Black students, four (Georgia, Florida, New York and Illinois) have lower than average male Black graduation rates. Among *districts* enrolling 10,000 or more male Black students, ten have higher male Black graduation rates than the national average. Two — Montgomery County (MD) and Newark—exceed the 2001/2 national male White, non-Hispanic, graduation rate. Philadelphia, Clark County, Detroit and Rochester, on the other hand, graduate less that a quarter of their male Black students. Six more districts graduate less than one-third. These wide variations in outcomes, against a nearly uniform background of family poverty, point again to educational opportunity — the quality of schools available—as the key to the educational challenges facing Black students.

These patterns continue at the postsecondary level. Twelve percent of male Black high school graduates enroll in two-year colleges and 31% in four-year colleges. In comparison, 23% of male White students enroll in two-year colleges and 41% in 4-year colleges.[22] If we look at these numbers more carefully, we see that most male Black high school graduates (57%) do not enroll in college at all, while two-thirds of male White students do so. These figures become even more dramatic when combined with high school graduation rates. Only half of male Black high school students graduate; approximately three-quarters of male White, non-Hispanic, students graduate. It would seem, then, that just six percent of college age male Black students enroll in two-year colleges and 16% enroll in four-year colleges, compared to 18% and 30% of male White students. In other words, a male White high school student is twice as likely as a male Black student to enroll in college following the year in which their cohort was in grade 12.

A degree-seeking, full-time, male Black student in a four-year college is half as likely to graduate in four years as a male White student (15% compared to 33%). However, by six years from enrollment, 36% of male Black students and 57% of male White students graduate. The gap is similar but the disproportionality has narrowed.

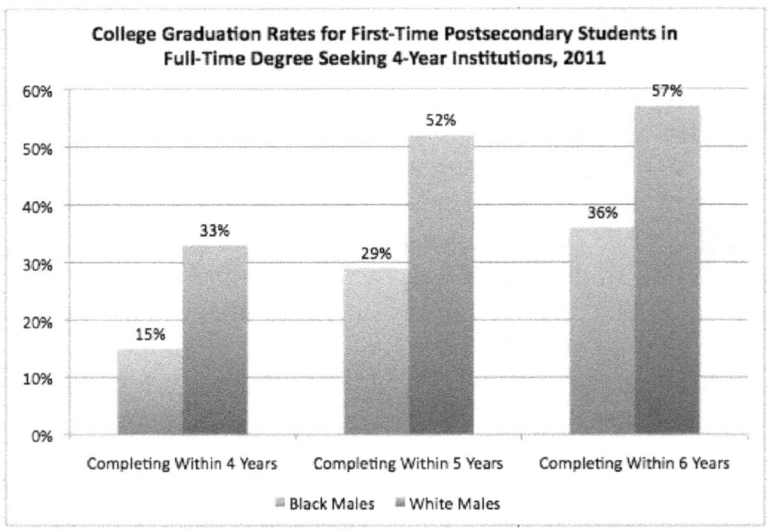

NCES; A Call For Change

An obvious interpretation of this data would point to a relative lack of adequate preparation for college coursework among those male Black students who have managed to obtain a high school diploma.

According to the Census Bureau's Community Population Survey (CPS), in terms of educational attainment, the largest group of White, non-Hispanic, men is that of those who have received a Bachelor's degree, while the largest group of Black men are those reporting just a high school diploma: four years less of education. While the percentages of those with some college or an Associate degree, combined, are identical (29%), just over one-third the percentage of African-American as White, non-Hispanic, men report receiving Bachelor's degrees and less than half the percentage of African-American as White, non-Hispanic, men report that they have been awarded graduate degrees. While twelve percent of White, non-Hispanic, men receive graduate degrees, only five percent of Black men do so.

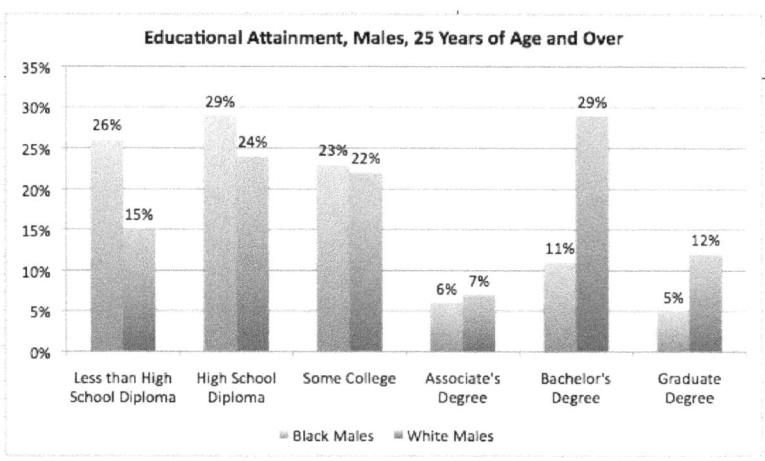

2010 Census

The percentage of African-American men receiving Bachelor's degrees, at 11%, according to the Census, is twice that which can be derived from the progression data described above. What accounts for this discrepancy? Professor Pettit has recently argued that because it does not include people in prison or jail, the Current Population Survey (CPS) seriously over-estimates the educational attainment of the Black population. Another factor in this over-estimation is the equation of the quality and timing of the GED with the high school diploma. There is some debate about the GED as literally equivalent to a high school diploma and, further, many male African-Americans receive their GED while incarcerated, which is quite a different matter than taking the examination as an alternative to sitting out the final semester of high school. The chart below follows Pettit in classifying reported GEDs with those having less than a high school diploma.

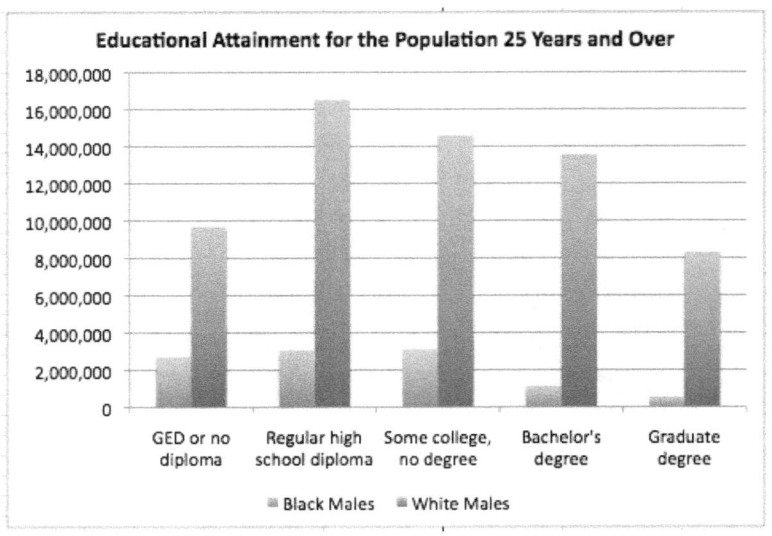

Assuming that Pettit is correct, the actual percentage of college educated African-American men is much lower than usually thought; the number of college educated African-American men, as compared to White, non-Hispanic, men, is barely noticeable; that of African-American men with graduate degrees hardly more than a rounding error for the combined total.

Half of those male Black students enrolled in grade 9 graduate from high school four years later. Less than a third of those then enroll in a four-year college. Slightly more than a third of those have graduated after six years. Approximately five percent, then, of a given cohort of male Black students go straight through to a Bachelor's degree, allowing for six years to complete the degree after matriculation. If the economic status of African-Americans is to approach the level of that for other Americans, it is essential that the percentage of African-Americans with college degrees doubles and for that it is essential that African-American children attend dramatically better schools than those most of them attend today.

Du Bois ended his account of the establishment of schooling for African-Americans during and immediately after

Reconstruction with a paean to what we would today call African-American *agency* during Jim Crow:

> Had it not been for the Negro school and college, the Negro would, to all intents and purposes, have been driven back to slavery. His economic foothold in land and capital was too slight in ten years of turmoil to effect any defense or stability … But already, through establishing public schools and private colleges, and by organizing the Negro church, the Negro had acquired enough leadership and knowledge to thwart the worst designs of the new slave drivers. They avoided the mistake of trying to meet force by force. They bent to the storm of beating, lynching and murder, and kept their souls in spite of pubic and private insult of every description; they built an inner culture which the world recognizes in spite of the fact that it is still half-strangled and inarticulate.[23]

The achievement Du Bois memorializes was indeed admirable, and, as he said, admired. But today more is needed. The closed gate to education opportunity for Black students is not controlled by the Black community. Dr. John H. Jackson has spoken of "the willful neglect" of educational opportunities for African-Americans. It is widely believed that it is the duty of the oppressed to struggle against oppression. Hence the admiration for Spartacus and his successors. But there is no moral law that the struggle against oppression, in whatever realm, must be carried on only by the oppressed, nor any historical analysis that holds that the struggling oppressed, on their own, must succeed in ending their oppression. The direct route to the end of oppression is for the oppressors themselves to work with the oppressed to end it. It is also the moral responsibility of those keeping the gate of educational opportunity closed to join hands with those behind it, to work together to remove that barrier to the fulfillment of the promise of Emancipation.

Appendix to Chapter III

TABLE 9

State Graduation Rates

A few states with small Black populations had graduation rates for their Black Male students higher than the national average graduation rate for White, non-Hispanic, male students. The District of Columbia, Nebraska, New York and Wisconsin had conspicuously large gaps between their graduation rates for Black and White Male students.[24]

State	Male High School Graduation Rate		Gap
	Black	White, non-Hispanic	
Alabama	53%	69%	15%
Alaska	71%	70%	-1%
Arizona	84%	82%	-2%
Arkansas	59%	73%	14%
California	56%	83%	26%
Colorado	56%	75%	19%
Connecticut	59%	85%	26%
Delaware	47%	68%	22%
District of Columbia	38%	88%	50%
Florida	47%	62%	15%
Georgia	49%	65%	17%
Hawaii	60%	39%	-21%
Idaho	73%	79%	6%
Illinois	47%	81%	34%
Indiana	49%	80%	31%
Iowa	41%	90%	49%
Kansas	54%	80%	27%
Kentucky	58%	69%	11%
Louisiana	49%	63%	14%
Maine	97%	86%	-11%
Maryland	57%	81%	24%

Massachusetts	60%	83%	23%
Michigan	54%	80%	25%
Minnesota	65%	89%	24%
Mississippi	51%	62%	11%
Missouri	56%	81%	25%
Montana	63%	82%	18%
Nebraska	44%	86%	43%
Nevada	52%	61%	8%
New Hampshire	60%	80%	20%
New Jersey	63%	90%	27%
New Mexico	49%	62%	13%
New York	37%	78%	42%
North Carolina	58%	71%	13%
North Dakota	*	91%	*
Ohio	45%	80%	35%
Oklahoma	64%	76%	12%
Oregon	72%	77%	5%
Pennsylvania	57%	85%	28%
Rhode Island	64%	75%	11%
South Carolina	46%	62%	16%
South Dakota	65%	81%	16%
Tennessee	62%	76%	13%
Texas	53%	75%	22%
Utah	76%	84%	7%
Vermont	82%	81%	-2%
Virginia	54%	77%	23%
Washington	55%	74%	19%
West Virginia	62%	69%	7%
Wisconsin	55%	92%	38%
Wyoming	59%	78%	19%
USA	**52%**	**78%**	**26%**

TABLE 10

Graduation Rates For Districts

Enrolling 10,000 or More Black Male Students

Estimated 2009/10 *district* four-year graduation rates for Black, Hispanic and White, non-Hispanic, male students, for districts enrolling 10,000 or more male Black students. Of the five districts with the highest graduation rates for Black males, two are in Maryland and two in North Carolina. Of the districts with the lowest graduation rates for male Black students, two are in New York State and two in Georgia.

District	Male High School Graduation Rate		
	Black	White	Gap
Atlanta (GA)	42%	73%	31%
Baltimore City (MD)	40%	43%	4%
Baltimore County (MD)	67%	79%	12%
Birmingham City (AL)	37%	46%	9%
Boston (MA)	50%	68%	18%
Broward County (FL)	52%	64%	12%
Caddo Parish (LA)	39%	58%	19%
Charleston (SC)	36%	67%	30%
Charlotte-Mecklenburg (NC)	44%	72%	28%
Chatham County (GA)	27%	42%	15%
Chicago (IL)	39%	66%	28%
Cincinnati (OH)	33%	49%	16%
Clark County (NV)	22%	37%	15%
Clayton County (GA)	35%	20%	14%
Cleveland (OH)	28%	37%	9%
Cobb County (GA)	52%	77%	24%

Columbus City (OH)	41%	43%	2%
Cumberland County (NC)	68%	69%	1%
Dallas (TX)	35%	50%	15%
DeKalb County (GA)	46%	72%	26%
Detroit (MI)	20%	7%	13%
District of Columbia	38%	88%	50%
Duval County (FL)	36%	53%	17%
East Baton Rouge Parish (LA)	42%	44%	2%
Fort Bend (TX)	60%	83%	23%
Fulton County (FL)	47%	83%	36%
Guilford County (NC)	67%	80%	13%
Gwinnett County (GA)	41%	61%	20%
Hillsborough County (FL)	47%	70%	23%
Houston (TX)	40%	73%	34%
Jackson (MS)	28%	42%	14%
Jefferson County (KY)	49%	53%	4%
Jefferson Parish (LA)	50%	56%	6%
Los Angeles (CA)	41%	64%	23%
Memphis (TN)	43%	67%	24%
Miami-Dade (FL)	49%	71%	22%
Milwaukee (WI)	45%	55%	10%
Mobile County (AL)	38%	49%	10%
Montgomery County (AL)	33%	50%	17%
Montgomery County (MD)	74%	91%	17%
Nashville-Davidson (TN)	47%	56%	9%
New York City (NY)	28%	57%	29%
Newark (NJ)	74%	67%	-7%
Norfolk (VA)	32%	52%	20%
Orange County (FL)	49%	67%	17%
Palm Beach County (FL)	55%	71%	16%
Philadelphia (PA)	24%	39%	14%

Pinellas County (FL)	34%	58%	24%
Polk County (FL)	46%	57%	11%
Prince George's County (MD)	55%	60%	5%
Richmond County (GA)	27%	32%	5%
Rochester (NY)	9%	31%	22%
St. Louis (MO)	33%	41%	8%
Virginia Beach (VA)	54%	72%	18%
Wake County (NC)	59%	85%	26%

TABLE 11

NAEP State Grade 8 Reading Scores

National Assessment of Educational Progress (NAEP), "the Nation's Report Card," measures student achievement at various grade levels in a variety of subject and skill areas. The following tables show the results of the 2011 NAEP for 8th Grade Reading, which is considered a good indicator of "value added" by schools.

| States | Percent at or Above Proficient | | Gap |
	Black Male	White, non-Hispanic Male	White/Black
Alabama	8%	30%	22%
Alaska	13%	34%	21%
Arizona	13%	35%	23%
Arkansas	6%	29%	23%
California	4%	27%	23%
Colorado	15%	43%	29%
Connecticut	19%	48%	29%
Delaware	13%	33%	21%
District of Columbia	8%	‡	-
Florida	10%	34%	24%
Georgia	10%	33%	23%
Hawaii	‡	33%	-
Idaho	‡	32%	-
Illinois	11%	38%	27%
Indiana	9%	31%	23%
Iowa	13%	30%	17%
Kansas	12%	36%	24%
Kentucky	11%	34%	23%
Louisiana	8%	26%	18%
Maine	‡	34%	-
Maryland	17%	45%	28%
Massachusetts	13%	48%	35%
Michigan	7%	29%	23%
Minnesota	12%	38%	27%
Mississippi	7%	27%	19%
Missouri	8%	33%	25%

Montana	‡	38%	-
Nebraska	7%	34%	27%
Nevada	11%	29%	18%
New Hampshire	‡	35%	-
New Jersey	12%	49%	37%
New Mexico	‡	30%	-
New York	15%	39%	24%
North Carolina	9%	33%	25%
North Dakota	‡	30%	-
Ohio	9%	38%	30%
Oklahoma	11%	25%	13%
Oregon	‡	33%	-
Pennsylvania	10%	39%	29%
Rhode Island	12%	35%	23%
South Carolina	6%	31%	25%
South Dakota	‡	33%	-
Tennessee	9%	26%	17%
Texas	12%	41%	29%
Utah	‡	34%	-
Vermont	‡	37%	-
Virginia	11%	37%	26%
Washington	12%	35%	22%
West Virginia	13%	19%	5%
Wisconsin	9%	34%	25%
Wyoming	‡	34%	-
USA	**10%**	**35%**	**25%**

‡ Indicates insufficient number of students for analysis.

TABLE 12

NAEP Selected District Grade 8 Reading Scores

NAEP measures achievement in selected urban areas, as well as the states. Austin, Boston (MA), Charlotte, Chicago (IL), Hillsborough County (FL), Houston (TX), Los Angeles (CA), Miami Date and San Diego show above average achievement levels for White male students. Boston (MA), Charlotte, Miami-Dade (FL) and New York City (NY) show above average achievement levels for Black male students.

States	Percent at or Above Proficient		Gap
	Black	White, non-Hispanic	White/ Black
Albuquerque	-	30%	-
Atlanta (GA)	9%	-	-
Austin	9%	49%	40%
Baltimore City (MD)	7%	-	-
Boston (MA)	10%	45%	35%
Charlotte-Mecklenburg (NC)	12%	50%	38%
Chicago (IL)	9%	36%	27%
Cleveland (OH)	3%	17%	14%
Dallas (TX)	7%	-	-
Detroit (MI)	5%	-	-
Fresno	-	22%	-
Hillsborough County (FL)	9%	39%	29%
Houston (TX)	9%	50%	40%
Jefferson County (KY)	9%	33%	24%
Los Angeles (CA)	9%	36%	27%
Miami-Dade (FL)	11%	41%	30%
Milwaukee (WI)	3%	21%	19%
New York City (NY)	13%	32%	19%
Philadelphia (PA)	9%	27%	18%
San Diego	7%	38%	31%
USA	**10%**	**35%**	**25%**

TABLE 13

NAEP State Grade 8 Mathematics Scores

8th Grade Mathematics achievement is a key predicator of success in high school graduation and college admission.

| States | Percent at or Above Proficient | | Gap |
	Black	White, non-Hispanic	White/ Black
Alabama	7%	30%	24%
Alaska	‡	49%	-
Arizona	14%	48%	34%
Arkansas	10%	38%	28%
California	9%	42%	33%
Colorado	20%	55%	35%
Connecticut	15%	49%	34%
Delaware	12%	42%	29%
District of Columbia	13%	‡	-
Florida	9%	38%	29%
Georgia	10%	41%	31%
Hawaii	‡	41%	-
Idaho	‡	42%	-
Illinois	10%	46%	36%
Indiana	11%	39%	28%
Iowa	‡	38%	-
Kansas	20%	48%	28%
Kentucky	14%	35%	21%
Louisiana	9%	31%	22%
Maine	‡	39%	-
Maryland	17%	59%	41%
Massachusetts	26%	58%	32%
Michigan	7%	37%	30%
Minnesota	17%	54%	37%
Mississippi	8%	28%	20%
Missouri	7%	38%	31%
Montana	‡	50%	-
Nebraska	8%	41%	34%
Nevada	16%	44%	27%
New Hampshire	‡	44%	-

New Jersey	22%	61%	39%
New Mexico	‡	41%	-
New York	11%	40%	29%
North Carolina	15%	49%	34%
North Dakota	‡	49%	-
Ohio	13%	47%	34%
Oklahoma	15%	34%	19%
Oregon	‡	40%	-
Pennsylvania	10%	49%	39%
Rhode Island	17%	43%	25%
South Carolina	13%	42%	29%
South Dakota	‡	48%	-
Tennessee	10%	31%	21%
Texas	18%	60%	41%
Utah	‡	43%	-
Vermont	‡	46%	-
Virginia	16%	49%	33%
Washington	11%	47%	36%
West Virginia	15%	23%	8%
Wisconsin	8%	49%	41%
Wyoming	‡	45%	-
USA	**12%**	**45%**	**33%**

TABLE 14

NAEP Selected District Grade 8 Mathematics Scores

Districts	Percent at or Above Proficient		Gap
	Black Male	White, non-Hispanic, Male	White/Black
Albuquerque	‡	43%	-
Atlanta (GA)	11%	70%	58%
Austin	‡	67%	-
Baltimore City (MD)	11%	‡	-
Boston (MA)	22%	56%	35%
Charlotte-Mecklenburg (NC)	14%	69%	55%
Chicago (IL)	9%	49%	40%
Cleveland (OH)	6%	29%	23%
Dallas (TX)	9%	‡	-
Detroit (MI)	3%	‡	-
District of Columbia	8%	‡	-
Fresno	7%	35%	27%
Hillsborough County (FL)	10%	44%	34%
Houston (TX)	15%	70%	55%
Jefferson County (KY)	13%	32%	19%
Los Angeles (CA)	8%	46%	38%
Miami-Dade (FL)	10%	43%	33%
Milwaukee (WI)	5%	20%	15%
New York City (NY)	10%	47%	37%
Philadelphia (PA)	13%	33%	21%
San Diego	9%	56%	48%
USA	**12%**	**45%**	**32%**

TABLE 15

Gifted and Talented Programs

Percentages of Male Students in Gifted and Talented Programs[25]

Districts	Black	White, non-Hispanic	White/ Black Ratio
Atlanta (GA)	5%	32%	7
Baltimore City (MD)	3%	5%	2
Baltimore County (MD)	12%	24%	2
Birmingham City (AL)	3%	11%	3
Boston (MA)	1%	3%	3
Broward County (FL)	2%	8%	5
Caddo Parish (LA)	1%	9%	8
Charleston (SC)	4%	26%	7
Charlotte-Mecklenburg (NC)	4%	21%	6
Chatham County (GA)	5%	19%	4
Chicago (IL)	1%	4%	3
Cincinnati City (OH)	2%	11%	6
Clark County (NV)	1%	3%	4
Clayton County (GA)	4%	7%	2
Cleveland City (OH)	4%	10%	2
Cobb County (GA)	5%	23%	5
Columbus City (OH)	2%	8%	5
Cumberland County	2%	8%	5
Miami-Dade (FL)	5%	21%	4
Dallas (TX)	7%	19%	3
DeKalb County (GA)	6%	34%	5
Detroit City (MI)	0%	0%	-
District Of Columbia	0%	0%	-
Duval County (FL)	1%	5%	6
East Baton Rouge Parish (LA)	2%	11%	6
Fort Bend (TX)	3%	13%	5
Fulton County (FL)	6%	30%	6
Guilford County (NC)	7%	29%	4
Gwinnett County (GA)	6%	23%	4
Hillsborough County (FL)	1%	6%	5

Houston (TX)	6%	37%	7
Jackson (MS)	6%	19%	3
Jefferson County (KY)	3%	10%	4
Jefferson Parish (LA)	3%	9%	3
Los Angeles (CA)	6%	23%	4
Memphis City (TN)	1%	6%	9
Milwaukee (WI)	4%	4%	1
Mobile County (AL)	4%	10%	3
Montgomery County (AL)	2%	5%	4
Montgomery County (MD)	42%	61%	1
Nashville-Davidson (TN)	2%	19%	9
Newark City (NJ)	4%	8%	2
Norfolk City (VA)	7%	23%	3
Orange County (FL)	1%	11%	7
Palm Beach County (FL)	1%	8%	7
Philadelphia City (PA)	2%	9%	4
Pinellas County (FL)	1%	7%	6
Polk County (FL)	2%	6%	3
Prince George's County (MD)	8%	26%	3
Richmond County (GA)	1%	4%	3
Rochester City (NY)	1%	2%	2
St. Louis City (MO)	1%	11%	8
Virginia Beach City (VA)	4%	15%	3
Wake County (NC)	5%	26%	5

Data from the U. S. Department of Education, Office for Civil Rights

119

TABLE 16

Percentages of Male Students Classified as

Intellectually Disabled

Districts	Black	White, non-Hispanic	Black/ White Ratio
Atlanta (GA)	1.49%	0.18%	8.3
Baltimore City (MD)	1.53%	1.30%	1.2
Baltimore County (MD)	0.80%	0.46%	1.7
Birmingham City (AL)	2.14%	4%	0.6
Boston (MA)	3.16%	1.71%	1.8
Broward County (FL)	1.33%	0.53%	2.5
Caddo Parish (LA)	2.53%	0.79%	3.2
Charleston (SC)	2.46%	0.69%	3.6
Charlotte-Mecklenburg (NC)	2.14%	0.66%	3.2
Chatham County (GA)	1.57%	0.51%	3.1
Chicago (IL)	2.31%	1.25%	1.9
Cincinnati (OH)	4.00%	2.20%	1.8
Clark County (NV)	0.61%	0.30%	2.0
Clayton County (GA)	1.23%	2.36%	0.5
Cleveland (OH)	4.11%	2.50%	1.6
Cobb County (GA)	1.00%	0.45%	2.2
Columbus	2.25%	2.00%	1.1
Cumberland County	2.09%	0.95%	2.2
Miami-Dade (FL)	1.66%	0.62%	2.7
Dallas (TX)	1.56%	0.85%	1.8
DeKalb County (GA)	1.58%	0.62%	2.5
Detroit (MI)	3.41%	3.43%	1.0
District of Columbia	1.89%	0.00%	-
Duval County (FL)	2.99%	1.29%	2.3
East Baton Rouge Parish (LA)	0.95%	0.57%	1.7
Fort Bend (TX)	1.23%	0.34%	3.6
Fulton County (FL)	1.07%	0.41%	2.6
Guilford County (NC)	1.68%	0.59%	2.9
Gwinnett County (GA)	1.14%	0.65%	1.8
Hillsborough County (FL)	2.77%	1.02%	2.7

Houston (TX)	1.56%	0.49%	3.2
Jackson (MS)	1.34%	0.00%	-
Jefferson County (KY)	3.60%	1.82%	2.0
Jefferson Parish (LA)	2.55%	1.21%	2.1
Los Angeles (CA)	1.04%	0.46%	2.2
Memphis (TN)	0.00%	0.00%	-
Milwaukee (WI)	2.72%	1.88%	1.4
Mobile County (AL)	1.21%	0.7%	1.7
Montgomery County (AL)	1.25%	-	3.6
Montgomery County (MD)	0.68%	0.38%	1.8
Nashville-Davidson (TN)	0.00%	0.00%	-
Newark (NJ)	0.49%	0.34%	1.5
Norfolk City (VA)	1.33%	0.97%	1.4
Orange County (FL)	2.81%	0.93%	3.0
Palm Beach County (FL)	1.93%	0.65%	3.0
Philadelphia (PA)	1.96%	1.53%	1.3
Pinellas County (FL)	2.57%	0.93%	2.8
Polk County (FL)	3.41%	1.59%	2.1
Prince George's County (MD)	0.88%	0.82%	1.1
Richmond County (GA)	2.22%	1.00%	2.2
Rochester (NY)	1.46%	1.20%	1.2
St. Louis (MO)	1.83%	0.00%	-
Virginia Beach (VA)	0.96%	0.45%	2.1
Wake County (NC)	2.01%	0.36%	5.6

U. S. Department of Education, Office for Civil Rights. "Intellectually Disabled" replaces the "Mentally Retarded" Special Education category formerly used in this table.

TABLE 17

Percentages of Male Students in

Advance Placement Mathematics Classes

Districts	Black	White, non-Hispanic	White/Black Ratio
Atlanta (GA)	0.70%	1.08%	1.5
Baltimore City (MD)	0.30%	0.72%	2.4
Baltimore County (MD)	0.77%	2.23%	2.9
Birmingham	0.19%	-	0.0
Boston (MA)	0.67%	1.71%	2.6
Broward County (FL)	0.24%	1.04%	4.3
Caddo Parish (LA)	0.07%	0.79%	10.6
Charleston (SC)	0.20%	1.27%	6.5
Charlotte-Mecklenburg (NC)	0.65%	3.52%	5.4
Chatham County (GA)	0.09%	0.51%	5.7
Chicago (IL)	0.28%	1.15%	4.1
Cincinnati (OH)	0.18%	1.16%	6.6
Clark County (NV)	0.26%	0.83%	3.2
Clayton County (GA)	0.26%	0.47%	1.8
Cleveland (OH)	0.10%	0.12%	1.2
Cobb County (GA)	0.66%	2.68%	4.1
Columbus	0.28%	0.62%	2.2
Cumberland County	0.48%	1.25%	2.6
Miami-Dade (FL)	0.35%	1.49%	4.3
Dallas (TX)	0.66%	2.82%	4.3
DeKalb County (GA)	0.52%	1.96%	3.8
Detroit City (MI)	0.15%	0.43%	2.9
District of Columbia	0.29%	1.64%	5.7
Duval County (FL)	0.41%	1.48%	3.6
East Baton Rouge Parish (LA)	0.17%	1.89%	10.9
Fort Bend (TX)	0.57%	2.83%	5.0
Fulton County (FL)	0.39%	3.31%	8.5
Guilford County (NC)	0.56%	2.66%	4.7
Gwinnett County (GA)	0.69%	2.52%	3.6
Hillsborough County (FL)	0.44%	1.74%	3.9

Houston (TX)	0.28%	1.59%	5.8
Jackson (MS)	0.23%	0.00%	0.0
Jefferson County (KY)	0.25%	1.08%	4.4
Jefferson Parish (LA)	0.11%	0.30%	2.8
Los Angeles (CA)	0.63%	1.50%	2.4
Memphis (TN)	0.25%	1.60%	6.3
Milwaukee (WI)	0.06%	0.16%	2.5
Mobile County (AL)	0.03%	-	0.0
Montgomery County (AL)	0.28%	-	0.0
Montgomery County (MD)	0.95%	3.76%	4.0
Nashville-Davidson (TN)	0.44%	1.28%	2.9
Newark (NJ)	0.19%	0.34%	1.8
Norfolk (VA)	0.46%	2.55%	5.6
Orange County (FL)	0.36%	1.93%	5.3
Palm Beach County (FL)	0.31%	1.92%	6.2
Philadelphia (PA)	4.02%	9.53%	2.4
Pinellas County (FL)	0.14%	1.33%	9.6
Polk County (FL)	0.18%	0.66%	3.7
Prince George's County (MD)	0.48%	1.80%	3.7
Richmond County (GA)	0.50%	1.14%	2.3
Rochester (NY)	0.14%	0.60%	4.2
St. Louis (MO)	0.28%	0.52%	1.9
Virginia Beach (VA)	0.63%	2.04%	3.2
Wake County (NC)	0.38%	2.68%	7.1

U. S. Department of Education, Office for Civil Rights.

The College Board advises that Advanced Placement (AP) classes should be open to all students, but admission to AP classes is at the discretion of local education authorities.

TABLE 18

Out-Of-School Suspensions

State Sample Suspension Risk for One or More Suspensions by
Race/Ethnicity 2009-2010 (Male and Female Combined)

State	Black	White, non-Hispanic	Black/White Ratio
Alabama	16.3	5.6	2.9
Alaska	10.9	4.5	2.4
Arizona	12.5	4.6	2.7
Arkansas	18.5	5.3	3.5
California	17.7	5.6	3.2
Colorado	13.9	4.3	3.2
Connecticut	20.4	2.4	8.5
Delaware	21.8	7.3	3.0
Georgia	17.1	4.9	3.5
Idaho	4.2	3.2	1.3
Illinois	25.3	3.9	6.5
Indiana	19.5	5.9	3.3
Iowa	13.9	3	4.6
Kansas	16.8	4	4.2
Kentucky	13.9	4.6	3.0
Louisiana	15.3	7	2.2
Maine	8.7	4.6	1.9
Maryland	11	4.9	2.2
Massachusetts	11.5	4.3	2.7
Michigan	22.1	6.2	3.6
Minnesota	17.6	2.3	7.7
Mississippi	17.6	6.4	2.8
Missouri	22.8	4.4	5.2
Montana	3.4	3.8	0.9
Nebraska	17.6	3.6	4.9
Nevada	22.6	8.2	2.8
New Hampshire	11.4	6.1	1.9
New Jersey	12	3.3	3.6
New Mexico	6.1	4.4	1.4
North Carolina	16.3	6.1	2.7
North Dakota	3.6	1.6	2.3
Ohio	18.6	4.6	4.0
Oklahoma	18.3	5.8	3.2
Oregon	12.5	4.9	2.6

Pennsylvania	16.7	3.6	4.6
Rhode Island	15.6	7	2.2
South Carolina	21	7.9	2.7
South Dakota	7.1	2.2	3.2
Tennessee	21.1	4.7	4.5
Texas	15.4	3.2	4.8
Utah	6.2	2.1	3.0
Vermont	6.5	4.4	1.5
Virginia	16.6	5	3.3
Washington	13.6	5.8	2.3
West Virginia	18.6	8.7	2.1
Wisconsin	18.5	3.2	5.8
Wyoming	13.8	10	1.4

From: Losen, Daniel J. and Jonathan Gillispie. Opportunities Suspended: The Disparate Impact of Disciplinary Exclusion from School. The Center for Civil Rights Remedies at The Civil Rights Project, August 2012. *Source:* CRDC, 2009-2010 (numbers from national sample rounded to one decimal).

Some states omitted because of data accuracy issues. MD and WI each had a large district removed from the sample so their estimates should be reviewed with extra caution.

Notes

---

[1] Myrdal, Gunnar. An American Dilemma: The Negro Problem and Modern Democracy. New York: Harper & Brothers Publishers, 1944, p. 887.

[2] Du Bois, W. E. B. Black Reconstruction: 1860-1880. New York: The Free Press, 1998, p. 638.

[3] Du Bois, p. 648.

[4] Du Bois, p. 649.

[5] Du Bois, p. 664.

[6] Du Bois, pp. 664-5.

[7] Myrdal, p. 896.

[8] Myrdal, p. 880.

[9] Du Bois, p. 695.

[10] Cox, Oliver C. Caste, Class and Race: A Study in Social Dynamics. New York: Modern Reader, 1970, p. 341.

[11] Orfield, John Kucsera and Genevieve Siegel-Hawley. E Pluribus . . . Separation: Deepening Double Segregation for More Students. The Civil Rights Project, September 2012.

[12] Myrdal, p. 901.

[13] Du Bois, pp. 662-3.

[14] Teachers College Record, Volume 116 Number 1, 2014, p. - http://www.tcrecord.org ID Number: 16889, Date Accessed: 10/21/2012 11:07:00 AM

[15] Teachers College Record, Volume 116 Number 1, 2014, p. - http://www.tcrecord.org ID Number: 16889, Date Accessed: 10/21/2012 11:07:00 AM

[16] Teachers College Record, Volume 87 Number 3, 1986, p. 356-373 http://www.tcrecord.org ID Number: 688, Date Accessed: 10/28/2011 1:44:58 PM

[17] Gilliam, W. S. (2005). Prekindergarteners left behind: Expulsion rates in state prekindergarten systems. New Haven, CT: Yale University Child Study Center.

[18] Fabelo, Tony et al., Breaking Schools' Rules: A Statewide Study of How School Discipline Relates to Students' Success and Juvenile Justice Involvement. 2011

[19] Much of the information in this chapter is from the 2012 Schott Foundation report *The Urgency of Now: The 2012 Schott 50 State*

Report on Public Education and Black Males. High school graduation rates are given as grade 9 enrollment divided by the number of regular diplomas issued four years later.

[20] See the recent Schott Foundation Report: *A Rotting Apple: Education Redlining in New York City.*

[21] The rulings in New Jersey's Abbott v. Burke case "cover 31 low-wealth, urban school districts, some of which, like Camden and Newark, are among the poorest in the United States. To ensure the children in these schools a "thorough and efficient" education, as required by the New Jersey Constitution, the Abbott rulings directed implementation of a comprehensive set of improvements, including adequate K-12 foundational funding, universal preschool for all 3- and 4-year old children, supplemental or at-risk programs and funding, and school-by-school reform of curriculum and instruction." See: http://www.edlawcenter.org/cases/abbott-v-burke.html

[22] Lewis, Sharon; Simon, Candace; Uzzell, Renata; Horwitz, Amanda; Casserly, Michael. A Call for Change: The Social and Educational Factors Contributing to the Outcomes of Black Males in Urban Schools. Council of Great City Schools, October, 2010.

[23] Du Bois, p. 667.

[24] Many numbers here and elsewhere in this report are rounded to the nearest whole number.

[25] Percentages and ratios in this and the following charts are rounded.

Chapter IV

Incarceration, Poverty and

The Educational Achievement of Male Black Students

"To make the society happy and people easy under the meanest circum-stances, it is requisite that great numbers of them should be ignorant as well as poor." Bernard Mandeville, *The Fable of the Bees.*

We have looked at incarceration rates, poverty and educational attainment for African-Americans, especially male African-Americans. These factors are not independent of one another. Mass incarceration of young adult African-American men leads to poverty for themselves and their families and is to some extent caused by that poverty (although to a great extent it is also caused by governmental policies and practices). Family poverty, given current fiscal policies in regard to education, usually confines Black children to schools where there is a little of educational opportunity. This in turn, giving the wheel another push, leads in the following years to reduced incomes, higher crime rates, shorter lives.

It is taken for granted that more Black than White children grow up in poverty. But why are more Black than White children growing up in poverty? Stopping the causal wheel at this question points to one important factor: a very large proportion of Black women raising children in poverty are doing so because the fathers of those children are imprisoned. Western and Pettit found that in 2009 over 11% of Black children had an incarcerated parent, as compared to fewer than 2% of White, non-Hispanic, and 3.5% of Hispanic children.[1] Pettit estimates that "one-quarter of black children will

129

experience parental imprisonment before their eighteenth birthday."[2] Black children, therefore, are between three and more than five times more likely than Hispanic or White, non-Hispanic, children to grow up without an adult male in or contributing to the household, simply because of the mass incarceration of Black men. The median family income of Black married couples with children was $70,000 in 2010. It was $21,500 for Black women raising children with no husband present—somewhat under the poverty line.[3] There are eleven million Black children under the age of 18. With 11% having an incarcerated parent, there are probably 1.2 million Black children, out of a total of the 3.9 million Black children living in poverty, who are living in poverty because their fathers are in prison. If the incarceration rate for African-American men were lowered to that for Hispanic men, for example, approximately 800,000 fewer Black children would grow up in poverty.

The intergenerational effects of the wheel of Black poverty are readily apparent at many points around its circumference. For example, the educational attainment—or lack thereof—of fathers is associated with that of their sons. The chart below shows the educational attainment of the fathers of male Black students, as reported by male Black students taking the NAEP Grade 8 Reading examination in 2011.

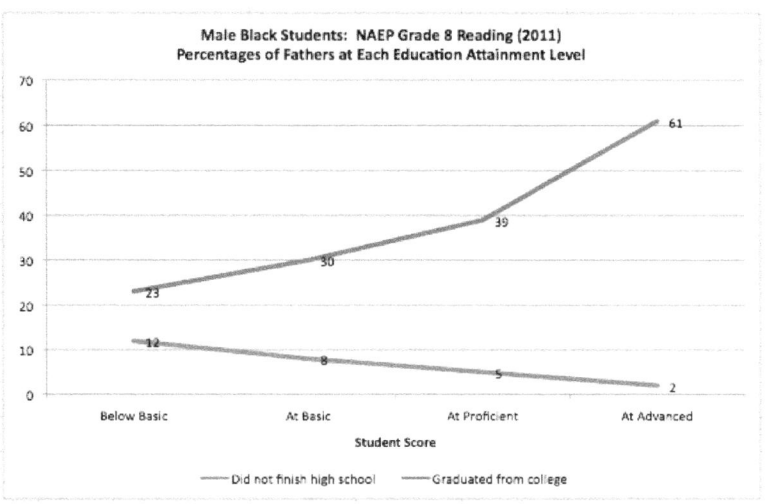

Twelve percent of those students scoring "below Basic" reported that their fathers had not finished high school, a percentage that declines as performance improves, so that only 2% of those scoring at the Advanced level reported that their fathers had not finished high school. The opposite was the case for those reporting that their fathers had completed college: 23% of those students scoring at the "below Basic" level report that their fathers had completed college, while 61% of those students scoring at the Advanced level reported that their fathers had completed college.[*] College educated fathers are relatively unlikely to have been incarcerated. They are likely to have higher incomes than those fathers who did not finish high school. Their sons will have the advantage of a parental model of commitment to education as well as the advantage of an upper middle class family income.

On average, just over half of African-American children from impoverished families, whose fathers did not finish high

---

[*] Thirty-two percent of male Black students scoring below Basic in grade 8 reported that they did not know their father's educational attainment (as compared to only 11% of those scoring at the Advanced level). It is not unlikely that most of those fathers would have either not finished high school or only reached a high school diploma or GED.

school score below grade level on the Grade 8 NAEP Reading assessment. Fifty-six percent of all *male* African-American students whose fathers did not finish high school score below grade level by grade 8. It can be assumed, then, from the relationship of income and incarceration, that more than half of those male Black children with incarcerated or formerly incarcerated fathers will themselves not graduate from high school.

The combination of poverty and parental incarceration inhibits educational attainment. U. C. Berkeley's Rucker C. Johnson has observed that "There are a myriad of ways in which parental incarceration may compound disadvantage.

> It may 1) increase the probabilities of growing up poor and/or with a single parent; or 2) elevate the risk of criminal involvement and incarceration later in life for children of the incarcerated ... There are a variety of potential mechanisms through which parental incarceration may affect child outcomes including economic instability, living-arrangement instability, parental attachment issues, role model effects, to name a few.[4]

Another way in which "parental incarceration may compound disadvantage," according to Johnson, is "neighborhood quality," which "is a significant gatekeeper of the intergenerational transmission of deviant behavior and incarceration risks among males."[5] In other words, children whose parents are in prison are likely to live in neighborhoods with deficient housing, inferior schools, high crime rates and an unusual degree of attention from the police. Part of the reason that these neighborhoods are of low quality is precisely because many of the men who might otherwise live in them are instead living in prison. Another reason is that many of the men who do live in them have been in prison and consequently have diminished economic prospects, among other disadvantages, such as an increased likelihood to have a place on a police list of usual suspects: to be arrested when arrests are needed to fill quotas, justify budgets, and the like.

In addition to the economic effects, the incarceration of a father can contribute to the prison to school to prison circuit by affecting the behavior of his children:

> One study found that 23 percent of children with a father who has served time in a jail or prison have been expelled or suspended from school, compared with just 4 percent of children whose fathers have not been incarcerated. Research that controls for other variables suggests that paternal incarceration, in itself, is associated with more aggressive behavior among boys and an increased likelihood of being expelled or suspended from school.[6]

Given eight million Black students enrolled k-12, and 25% with parents who have been incarcerated during their school years, then half a million Black children, overwhelmingly male, can be expected to be suspended or expelled from school simply from the effects of parental incarceration. These effects become apparent early in the school careers of Black children. Research by Christopher Wildeman "demonstrates that recent and prior paternal incarceration is associated with significantly higher levels of physically aggressive behaviors in boys at age five."[7] The immense number of arrests and incarcerations of Black men in contexts where White men would not be arrested or incarcerated may reduce the tolerance of Black children, especially male Black children, for the exercise of adult authority characteristic of schooling. Then the likelihood of a male Black student acting in such a way as to invoke school disciplinary procedures may be increased. On the other hand, as we have seen, other things being equal, just as Black males are disproportionately incarcerated, so Black male school children are disproportionately selected for school discipline actions. It is not necessarily the student's psychology that is primary in school discipline matters; it is often the psychology of the adult school authorities.

Incarceration of large numbers of young adult Black males affects the educational attainment of the mothers of their children as well. Assuming that, in general, families with incarcerated (or formerly incarcerated) fathers have low incomes, the following chart shows mothers' educational attainment for Black children from low-income (eligible for the National Lunch Program) and higher income (ineligible) families:

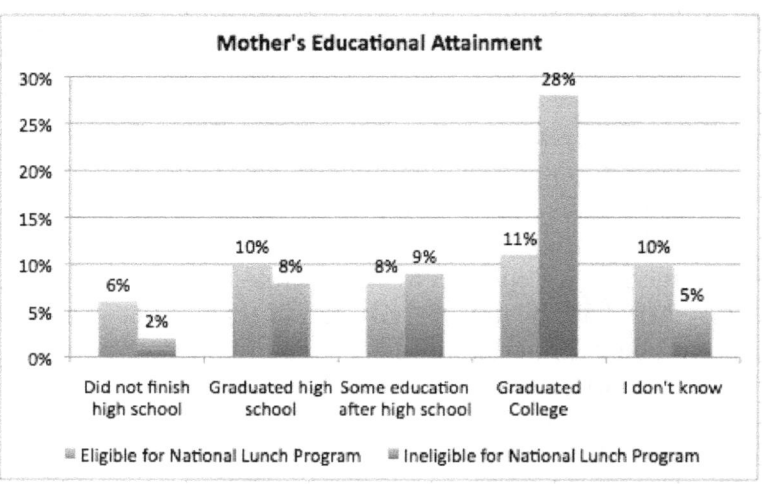

U. S. Department of Education, National Center for Education Statistics, National Assessment of Educational Progress, 2011

Four times the percentage Black students from lower income families as those from higher income families have mothers who were reported by their children as not having finished high school. Nearly three times the percentage of Black grade 8 students from higher income families than those from lower income families had mothers who graduated from college. Just 11% of Black students from low-income families report that their mothers graduated from college, while 28% of Black students from higher income families had college educated mothers. Fourteen times as many students from higher income families reported that their mothers graduated from college than that their mothers did not finish high school.

Looking at statistics such as these, Pamela Oliver and her colleagues note that "States with higher Black male imprisonment exhibit a rise in the prevalence of Black mothers — especially single mothers — who have not completed high school, despite an overall trend toward rising education among

Black women …

It seems likely that there are two mechanisms contributing to this result. One is the reduced legitimacy of mainstream institutions caused by perceptions of injustice and the rise in connections to criminal culture. The second is the rising competition for increasingly scarce men. On the first side, mass incarceration is associated with higher levels of community connections with prisoners and criminal lifestyles. Moreover, as the proportion of young men in a community incarcerated rises, the criminal justice system is seen increasingly as illegitimate by its targets, and this contributes to a general decline in the perceived legitimacy of the dominant culture. Young people of both sexes are pulled out of school by the disruptions in family life from having incarcerated relatives and by their own involvement in illegitimate or illegal activities. For a young woman, the paths to dropping out of high school and having a child are intertwined, as detachment from school and increasing sexual activity tend to reinforce each other. This leads to the second mechanism. While a steep reduction in the pool of available young men may lead some young women to defer sexual involvement and obtain more education, it can also lead others to be more willing to be sexually involved in the competition for increasingly scarce partners.[8]

This directly affects the educational achievement of male Black students, as the educational achievement of male Black students strongly tracks the reported educational attainment of their mothers as well as that of their fathers.

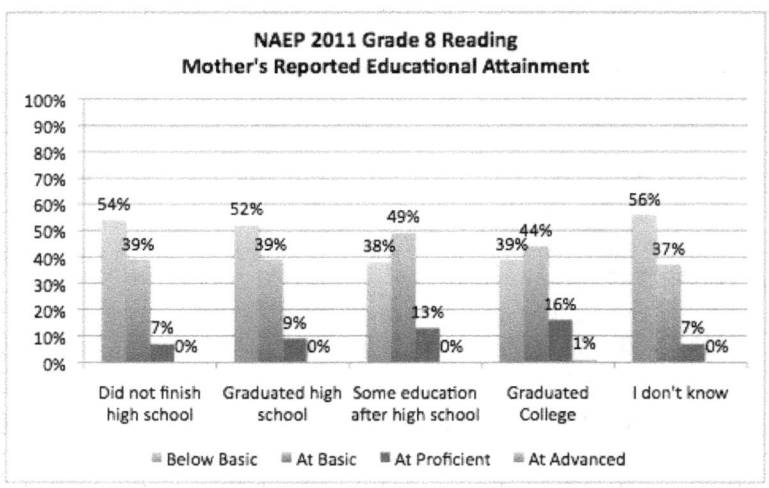

The percentage of male Black students scoring at or above Proficient more than doubles as their mothers' reported educational attainment increases. (As with the reported educational attainment of fathers, the percentages of male Black students reporting "I don't know" for mothers declines as scores rise.)

In the United States, as in many other countries, the dire effects of poverty on student learning begin well before children go to school. For example, in Australia, all children, without regard to race or ethnicity, "at four to five years of age from low-income families showed lower school readiness over all domains, but particularly in the area of language development. Two years later, at six to seven years of age, more children from low-income families were experiencing literacy and numeracy difficulties than children from middle income families."[9] Experience in the United States is similar. It is likely that due to the cumulative effects of family poverty, parental incarceration and multi-generational education deficiencies, as many as three-quarters of male Black children arrive at kindergarten unready for easy adaption to school routines and unready to begin learning basic literacy. In Maryland, in the 2001-2 school year (before the institution of the state's path-breaking school readiness program), approximately half of all kindergarten students were school-ready, but only 32% of all low-income students were judged to be school-ready. It is not surprising, then, that at that time only 35% of African-American students in Maryland, where a quarter of all Black children under five years of age lived in low-income families, were school-ready when they reached kindergarten.

Of course family poverty continues to affect student learning once children are enrolled in school. This can be illustrated with scores on the 2011 NAEP assessment of fourth grade Reading, comparing all students eligible for the National Lunch Program and all those ineligible, as determined by family income:

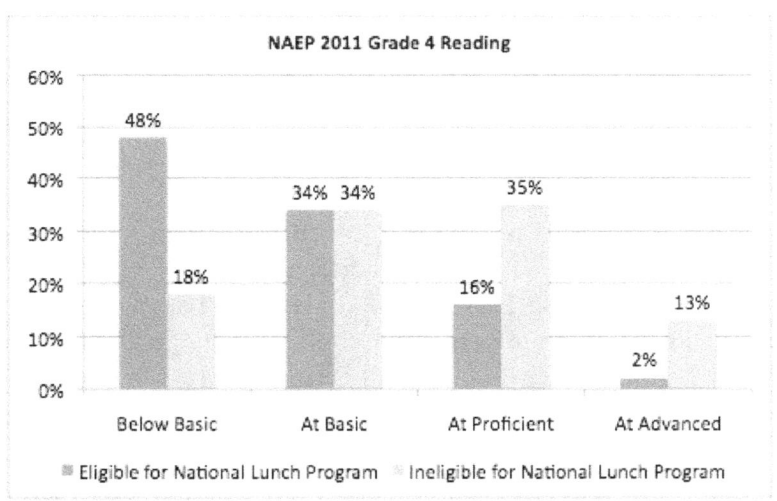

At the point in a student's school career that it is vital that their reading skills are at least at grade level, nearly half of those living in low-income households are reading far below grade level and an additional one-third have only Basic reading skills. Just one-sixth the proportion of students from low-income families as students from higher income families reach the Advanced level in grade 4 Reading.

Results from the grade 8 Reading assessment show that four more years of schooling decrease the percentage of students at the below Basic level who are low-income families, but only by increasing the percentage of those at the Basic level. The percentage of those reading at grade level (Proficient and above) is unchanged:

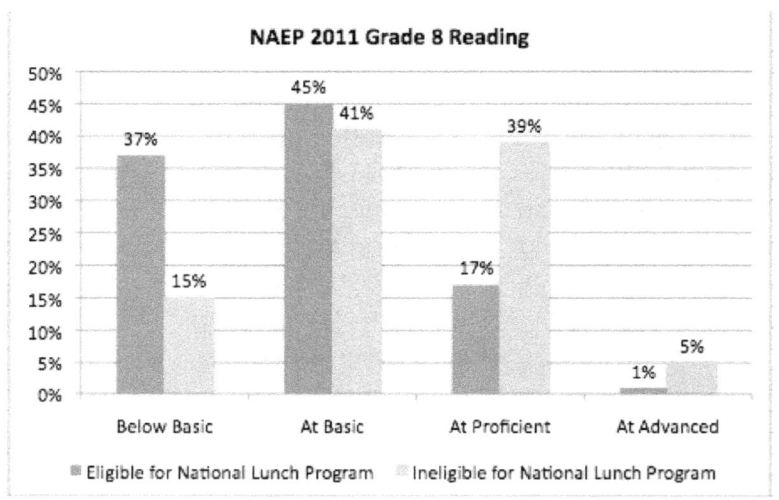

These poverty effects common to all American students are intensified among African-American students, particularly Black males. Young Black male students whose families have incomes sufficiently low to make them eligible for the National Lunch Program (nearly half of all Black children) rarely read at grade level by grade 4. Only 10% have skills that are Proficient or Advanced. On the other hand, three times that proportion, 29%, of male Black children from less impoverished households, read at grade level in grade 4.

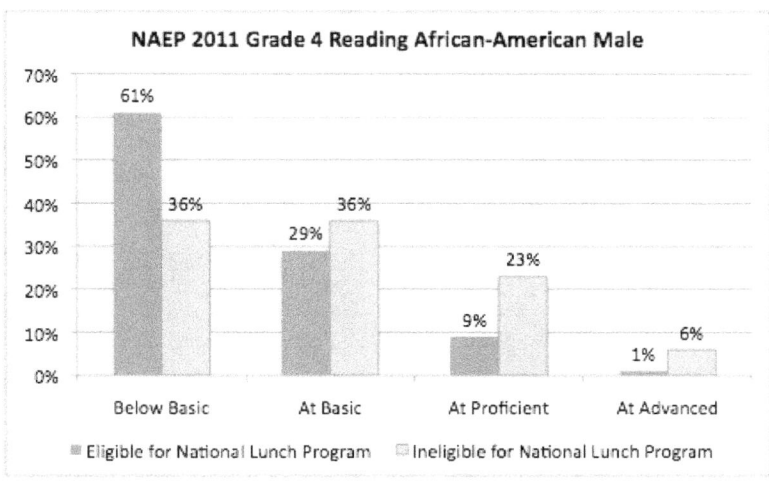

The deficient reading skills of low-income Black male students in primary school is of obvious importance. According to one researcher, Donald Hernandez, risk factors for failure to graduate from high school by age 19 include lack of reading proficiency in early elementary grades. (The other risk factors are the overlapping categories of poverty and "Black or Hispanic racial/ethnic status.")[10]

Percent Failing to Graduate from High School by Age 19, for Children by Third-Grade Reading Test Scores, by Race-Ethnicity, and by Poverty Experience					
			Reading Scores Below Proficiency		
	All Children	Proficient	Total	Basic	Below Basic
Total	12	4	16	9	23
White	9	4	13	7	19
Black	21	6	24	15	30
Hispanic	21	9	25	12	33
Have Not Experienced Poverty					
Total	6	2	9	5	14
White	5	2	7	4	12
Black	10	3	12	6	18
Hispanic	12	5	15	5	24
Have Experienced Poverty					
Total	22	11	26	18	31
White	19	11	22	15	27
Black	28	10	31	22	35
Hispanic	30	14	33	20	40

Hernandez, 2011.

Among White, non-Hispanic, children, 26% of those from low-income families and 51% of those from higher income families score at or above Proficient in Reading at grade 4, and virtually the same proportions, 25% and 47% do so at grade 8. On the other hand, 10% of those Black males from low-income families and 18% of those from higher income families score at or above Proficient at grade 4, while at grade 8 there has been no improvement: just 9% of those from low-income families and 19% of those from higher income families. The racial gap remains virtually the same. Ninety-one percent of male Black students in middle school from low-income families do not read at grade level. The same is true of 81% of middle class male Black middle school students. An argument can be made that reading achievement in the primary grades is predominately influenced by home factors. This argument is much less persuasive for middle school students. Their schools have had at least eight years to level the playing field. If they have not, the fault is most likely in the schools, not the families.

As we have seen, by and large, economically impoverished and middle class Black students attend the same schools. In a classic article, Russell Rumberger stated that: "not only are black and Hispanic children more likely to be poor, they are also more likely to attend schools with other poor children. In 2000, the average black or Hispanic student attended a school in which over 44% of students were poor, whereas the average white student attended a school in which 19% of the students were poor."[11] The lack of sufficient educational attainment by male Black children living in poverty might be attributed to family effects, including that of poverty itself, but what is the explanation for the almost as severe lack of educational attainment for many higher income male Black children? Part of the answer is that as the Black community is impoverished by the incarceration of large numbers of its young adult males, due to the segregated housing patterns of cities such as New York and Chicago, increasing percentages of the children in the Black community live in neighborhoods of, and attend schools with, concentrated poverty, without regard to their own family incomes.[12] More than 60% of Black students attend schools where more than half of the school population is identified as living in poverty, compared to 18% of White, non-Hispanic, students.[13] Recent studies of the "resegregation" of America indicate that many higher income Black families must live in these neighborhoods of concentrated poverty and their children to attend the same schools as those attended by the children of impoverished families. For example, while a third of the Black households in Brooklyn have incomes at or below the poverty level for a family of four, thirteen percent of the Black households in the borough have incomes at or above $100,000 per year, their children likely attending the same schools as those attended by the children of their impoverished neighbors.

A study by the Poverty & Race Research Action Council of characteristics of schools nearest to the homes of families at various income levels is suggestive in this regard.[14] The following table from that report compares proficiency in Mathematics and English Language Arts to a measure of family income.

Table 3. Median Characteristics of Schools Nearest to Housing Choice Voucher Households and Other Households with Children, by Race		
USA	Proficiency Percentile Rank Math/ELA	% Free/Reduced Price Lunch
White Housing Choice Voucher Households	40	56.6%
Black Housing Choice Voucher Households	20	80.7%
Hispanic Housing Choice Voucher Households	25	79.8%
All White Households	65	31.9%
All Black Households	24	76.5%
All Hispanic Households	34	74.0%
Poor White Households	47	51.6%
Poor Black Households	17	83.3%
Poor Hispanic Households	27	81.5%

While the median rank of the nearest school attended by children from all White households is 65% (and the percentage of children in those schools eligible for Free or Reduced Price Lunch is 31.9%), schools attended by children from poor White households are at a median proficiency percentile rank of 40 and a poverty rate of 51.6%. For all Black children the median percentile rank of the nearest school is 20, with a poverty rate of 76.5%, while for children from poor Black households, the median rank of the nearest school is 17, with a poverty rate of 83.3%. In other words, there is a 25 point difference in school quality rank for White children between that for all White children and that for poor White children, with a 20% difference in poverty levels, while for Black children the spread is just 3 points in quality and 7% in poverty.

It might not much matter that Black students, poor or not—although most are poor—attend schools where most of the other students are members of low-income families, if the quality of education provided by schools were not linked to average family income. But as we have seen, those schools, with exceptions of course, are under present conditions most likely to be less-well resourced than other schools, offering fewer opportunities to learn. The key indicator NAEP grade 8 Reading score illustrates this: it declines steeply as the percentage of students in a school who are from impoverished families increases.

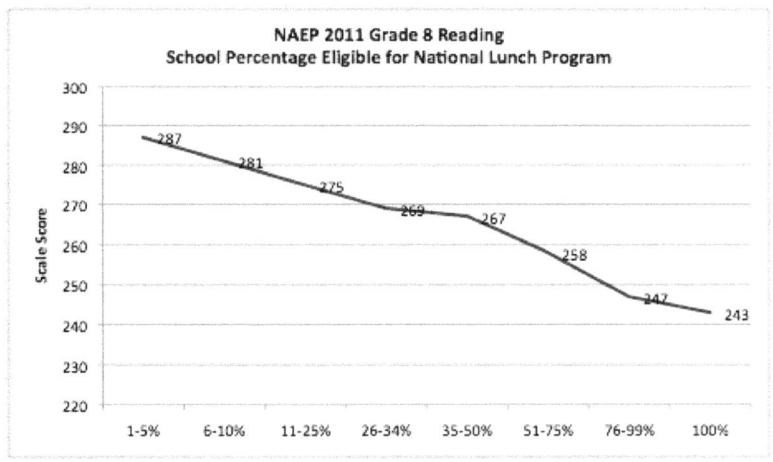

The following chart tests the relative influence of family and neighborhood economic status by showing levels of student achievement (percentage at or above Proficient on NAEP Grade 8 Reading) for students from low-income families and those from higher income families by the percentage of low-income students in the school:

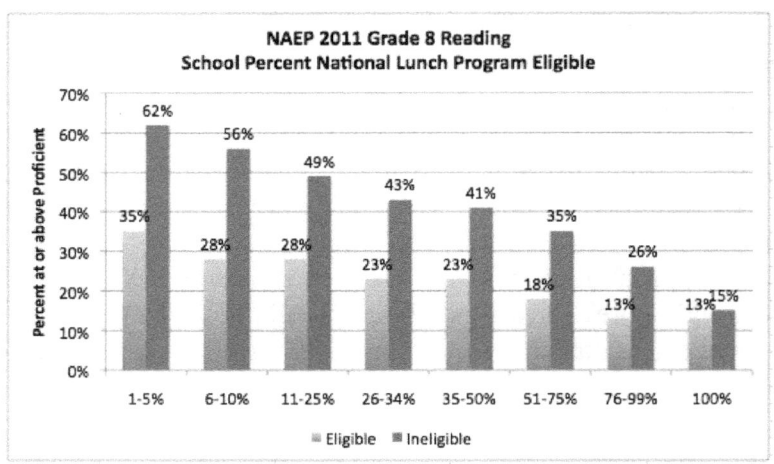

As the percentage of students in the school from low-income families increases (horizontal scale), the percentages of students, from both low-income and higher income families, scoring at or above Proficient declines. At 76% to 99% low-income, the percentage of those from higher income families scoring at or above Proficient is lower than that for students from low-income families in schools less than 10% poor. And, similarly, the percentage of students from low-income families attending schools in which just 5% or fewer of the students are also from low-income families scoring at or above Proficient is nearly three times that of similar students attending schools at the opposite end of the income scale, where 90% or more of the students are poor. Black students at grade 8 in schools that have low percentages of students from low-income families, and are themselves students from middle class families, are twice as likely to score at Proficient as are similar students in schools with high percentages of students from low-income families (36% v. 14%), reaching levels close to the national averages for all students from higher income families (38% Proficient and Advanced v. 44%). Black students from low-income families also benefit (19% v. 9% Proficient). Thus, the determining economic factor for student achievement appears to be not the economic status of the student's family alone, but also that of the school—that is, the average economic status of

144

the school's students.

In a word, schools serving high percentages of students from relatively impoverished families are not as good as schools serving low percentages of such students.

Why is that?

A study by Jonathan Rothwell for the Brookings Institution's Metropolitan Policy Program has demonstrated a strong connection among "Housing Costs, Zoning, and Access to High-Scoring Schools." Rothwell concludes that: "Nationwide, the average low-income student attends a school that scores at the 42nd percentile on state exams, while the average middle/high-income student attends a school that scores at the 61st percentile on state exams. This school test-score gap is even wider between black and Hispanic students and white students." [15] This is illustrated by the following chart:

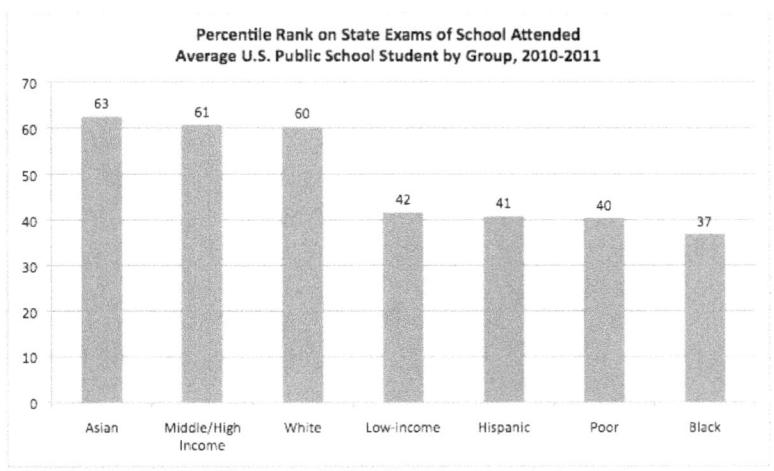

Adapted from Rothwell.

According to Rothwell's research, the average Asian or White and middle/high income student attends a school with a percentile ranking of 60 or better on state examinations, while the average Black student attends a school with a percentile ranking of 37, below that of the average student from a poor (below low-income) family.[†]

Why are schools the students of which are predominately low-income inadequate to their purpose? There are complex reasons and subtle arguments that can be deployed to answer this question. However, there is one cause for the condition of these schools that is obvious and readily apparent: American schools, virtually alone in the developed world, are funded by local property taxes. It is as if the motto of our public schools were "from each according to their wealth and *to* each according to their wealth (or lack thereof)." The consequences of this undemocratic distribution of resources are evident in nearly every aspect of American education.

Schools attended for the most part by students whose families are not in need of the National Lunch Program are usually in prosperous neighborhoods with relatively (or absolutely) expensive housing and relatively high property tax revenues.[‡] These schools—or rather their students—on average do well on the standardized tests used to rate schools and sell houses. One could imagine a world in which a family's financial poverty did not impoverish the educational opportunities of its children, but that imaginary world is nothing like the reality in this country today. American neighborhoods are increasingly segregated by income. Families living in poverty must in most places, send their children to underfinanced and therefore educationally impoverished schools. According to a recent U. S. Department of Education study by Ruth Heuer and Stephanie Stullich of Title I schools (i.e., those serving high percentages of students from

---

[†] There is strong evidence that low-income students receive life-long benefits from attending higher-scoring schools. Rothwell found that "For a young black adult, living in a metro area where blacks attend high-scoring schools is associated with $3,000 in extra income compared to a young black adult living in a metro where blacks attend low-scoring schools."

[‡] Not necessarily relatively high tax rates. Obviously more highly assessed property yields greater amounts of tax revenue at rates equal to or lower than those levied on less expensive property.

impoverished families): "42 percent to 46 percent of Title I schools (depending on school grade level) had per-pupil personnel expenditure levels that were below their district's average for non–Title I schools at the same grade level, and from 19 percent to 24 percent were more than 10 percent below the non–Title I school average."[16] In other words, nearly half the schools serving students from impoverished households received less funding from their district than those serving students from more prosperous households and nearly a quarter of those had per-student-expenditures significantly lower. "Similar patterns were found when comparing higher-poverty and lower-poverty schools within districts . . .

> Other expenditure categories examined in this study showed an increase in the percentage of Title I schools with below-average expenditure levels, compared with total non-personnel expenditures. At the elementary level, for example, the percentage of Title I schools that had per-pupil expenditures below their district's average for non–Title I schools at the same grade level was 46 percent for total personnel expenditures, 49 percent for instructional staff expenditures, 50 percent for teacher salary expenditures, and 54 percent for non-personnel expenditures.

Heuer and Stullich conclude with the observation that "It is worth noting that in some districts, a higher level of state and local resources were directed to Title I and higher-poverty schools relative to more advantaged schools in those districts. The example of these districts suggests that directing a higher level of state and local resources to high-need schools is an achievable goal." Or to put it another way, the decision to relatively underfund schools serving students living in poverty is discretionary: district administrations and boards of education choose to do so.

The Center for American Progress has recently published a paper by Ary Spatig-Amerikaner *(Unequal Education: Federal Loophole Enables Lower Spending on Students of Color),* in which Spatig-Amerikaner has used the newly available database of actual state and local spending on school-level personnel and non-personnel resources analyzed by federal researchers Heuer and Stullich to show that "schools with 90 percent or more students of color spend a full $733 less per student per year than schools with 90 percent or more white students ... On average, the high-minority schools ... would see an annual increase of $443,000 in state and local spending if [they] were brought up to the same per-pupil spending level as those schools with very few nonwhite students. This is enough to pay the average salary for 12 additional first-year teachers or nine veteran teachers." [17] Spatig-Amerikaner attributes these differentials in per pupil instructional spending to "maldistribution of resources at the district level ... Districts have teacher assignment practices that place the least-experienced teachers in high-minority, high-poverty schools. Because novice teachers earn so much less in salary, the total spending at these high-needs schools is likely to be lower than spending at schools in wealthier neighborhoods that employ veteran teachers" (p. 14).

Heuer and Stullich found that there is a relationship (inverse) between the percentage of Title I eligible schools and funding. Spatig-Amerikaner shows that there is a direct relationship between the racial composition of schools and instructional expenditures. This holds both between districts and within districts. The relationship, unsurprisingly, is that as Black student enrollment rises, instructional expenditures decline. As did the Schott Foundation's study of New York City schools (*A Rotting Apple: Education Redlining in New York City*), Spatig-Amerikaner derives the decline in expenditures from an analysis of the experience and educations of teachers. Using Spatig-Amerikaner's national data we can chart average per-student-expenditure against the percentage of Black students in schools. The following chart adds to that data the percentage of Black students scoring at or above Proficient on the NAEP Grade 8 Reading test.

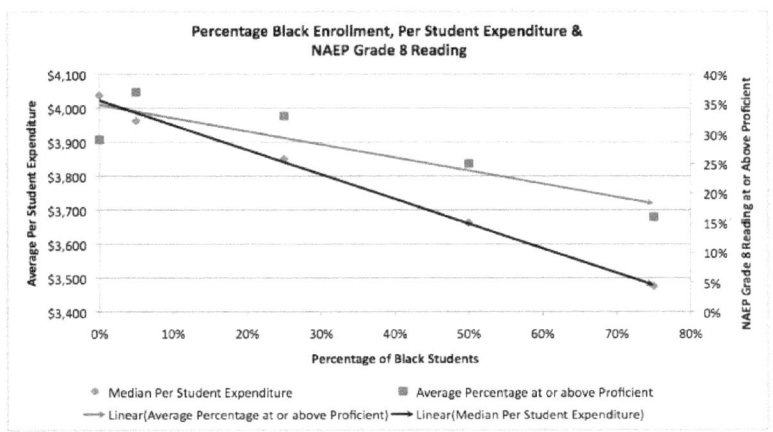

As the percentage of Black students (horizontal scale) rises, the per-student expenditure decreases, as does the percentage of Black students scoring at or above Proficient on the NAEP grade 8 Reading test. The level of per-student-expenditures is a direct measure of the opportunity to learn from more highly experienced, better-educated teachers.

The findings of Heuer and Stullich, Spatig-Amerikaner, the Schott Foundation and others demonstrate that, by and large, school funding in the United States is radically unfair: higher for the children of higher income, especially White, non-Hispanic, families and lower for the children of lower income, especially Black, families. The households of most African-American children are poor. Because they are poor they are likely to live in neighborhoods of concentrated poverty. High poverty neighborhood schools are likely to be disproportionately staffed by inexperienced, less-well-educated and younger, less-well-paid teachers. Student educational achievement in such schools is less that that of students in low-poverty schools, without regard to the income level of any given student's family. It is against this background that New Jersey's Education Law Center has established a set of core "fairness principles" for school funding. These include:

- Varying levels of funding are required to provide equal educational opportunities to children with different needs.

- The level of funding should increase relative to the level of concentrated student poverty. That is, state finance systems should provide more funding to districts serving larger shares of students in poverty ...
- Student poverty — especially concentrated student poverty — is the most critical variable affecting funding levels... State finance systems should deliver greater levels of funding to higher-poverty versus lower-poverty settings, while controlling for differences in other cost factors.[18]

They rarely do.

The circuit of Black poverty passes through the mass incarceration of young adult Black men based on decisions of police, district attorneys, judges and legislators; the consequent impoverishment of Black families; the resegregation of metropolitan areas and therefore of schools; the underfunding of segregated schools resulting in a lack of educational opportunity for Black students; lower educational attainment for young Black adults, leading to poverty and incarceration. None of this is necessary; little of it is entirely within the power of the Black community to stop. But it can be ended any day by those who have made, who continue to make, the decisions that cause Black poverty: members of boards of education, chief state school officers, school district superintendents, legislators, police department administrators, district attorneys, judges.

Notes

[1] Western, Dr. Bruce and Dr. Becky Pettit. Collateral Costs: Incarceration's Effect on Economic Mobility. Washington, DC: The Pew Charitable Trusts, 2010, p. 20

[2] Pettit, Becky. Invisible Men: Mass Incarceration and the Myth of Black Progress. New York: Russell Sage Foundation, 2011, p. 9.

[3] U. S. Census, 2006-2010 American Community Survey, B19126.

[4] Johnson, Rucker C. Intergenerational Risks of Criminal Involvement and Incarceration. April 2007.

[5] Johnson, Rucker C. Intergenerational Risks of Criminal Involvement and Incarceration. April 2007, p. 53)

[6] Western and Pettit, p. 21.

[7] Pettit, , p. 90.

[8] The Effect of Black Male Imprisonment on Black Child Poverty. Oliver, Pamela E. Gary Sandefur, Jessica Jakubowski, and James E. Yocom, p. 13.

[9] Hilferty, Fiona, The Implications of Poverty on Children's Readiness to Learn. Australian Rsearch Alliance for Children & Youth, 2009.

[10] Hernandez, Donald J. Double Jeopardy: How Third-Grade Reading Skills and Poverty Influence High School Graduation. The Annie E. Casey Foundation, April 2011.

[11] Rumberger, Russell W. Parsing the Data on Student Achievement in High-Poverty Schools. North Carolina Law Review, 85 (2007), 101-119.

[12] According to the Bureau of the Census, nearly half of African Americans live in "poverty areas," areas where poverty rates are 40% and above. Just seventeen percent of Whites live in such areas. See: Bishaw, Alemayehu. Areas with Concentrated Poverty: 2006-2010. American Community Survey Briefs, December, 2011.

[13] Orfield, G. and Lee, C. (2005). *Why segregation matters: Poverty and educational inequality*. Cambridge, MA: The Civil Rights Project at Harvard University.

[14] Ellen, Ingrid Gould and Horn, Keren Mertens. Do Federally Assisted Households Have Access to High Performing Public Schools. Poverty & Race Research Action Council. Civil Rights Research, November 2012.

[15] Rothwell, Jonathan. Housing Costs, Zoning, and Access to High-Scoring Schools. Brookings Institution, April 2012. http://www.brookings.edu/~/media/Files/rc/papers/2012/0419_school_inequality_rothwell/0419_school_inequality_rothwell.pdf

[16] Heuer, Ruth and Stephanie Stullich. Comparability of State and Local Expenditures Among Schools Within Districts: A Report from the Study of School-Level Expenditures. U.S. Department of Education, Office of Planning, Evaluation and Policy Development, Policy and Program Studies Service, 2011, p. 29.

[17] Spatig-Amerikaner, Ary. Unequal Education: Federal Loophole Enables Lower Spending on Students of Color. Center for American Progress, August 2012.

[18] Baker, Bruce, David Sciarra and Danielle Farrie. Is School Funding Fair? A National Report Card. Education Law Center, New Jersey. Second edition: June 2012, pp. 5-6.

Chapter V

Ending Black Poverty

"White prejudice and discrimination keep the Negro low in standards of living ... This, in turn, gives support to prejudice..." Gunner Myrdal[1]

To summarize this book's argument to this point:

In 2011the poverty rate for Black families with children under the age of 18 was 33%, that for White, non-Hispanic, families was less than half the Black poverty rate: 15%.[*] The difference can be attributed to the concentration of Black children in poorly resourced neighborhood schools and the mass incarceration of young adult Black men. Concentrated poverty, under conventional school funding policies, results in many Black students attending inadequately performing schools, schools that do not have the resources needed by children growing up in poverty. Large numbers of those children leave school without a high school diploma and young Black men without high school diplomas go to jail in inordinate numbers. The inordinate rates of incarceration of African-American men lead to disproportionate levels of Black poverty and disproportionate concentrations of Black neighborhood poverty foster disproportionate rates of violence, leading to yet higher rates of incarcerations for African-American men.

There is a large and growing scholarly and popular literature on a "school to prison pipeline" for young Black men. The argument of that literature is that lack of educational achievement and attainment among young Black men —

---

[*] The issue of Hispanic family poverty, which is nearly as high as that for African-American families, is primarily an artifact of issues of language and parental education.

together with such practices as extraordinary rates of out-of-school suspensions — lead to mass incarcerations of young adult Black men. Becky Pettit, for example, observes that "The education system contributes to particularly high dropout rates for black men, who then face a high risk of incarceration. As a result, incarceration has become a normative life course event for low-skill black men."[2] Pettit's book, *Invisible Men,* makes the argument that matters in regard to the educational attainment levels of African-American men are even worse than usually thought, as they have been distorted by a systematic downward bias in estimates of the high school dropout rate of male Black students (and thus an overestimate of their high school graduation rates). The source of this distortion is the convention of excluding prison inmates from census estimates. (If the size of a population group as a whole is underestimated, but the number of those attaining higher education credentials remains the same, the higher education attainment rate will be overestimated.) If this distortion is corrected, Pettit argues, "Including inmates in estimates suggests a nationwide high school dropout rate among young black men more than 40 percent higher than conventional estimates using the CPS [U. S. Census Current Population Survey] would suggest, and no improvement in the black-white gap in high school graduation rates since the early 1990s."[3]

Moving on to an estimate of how her corrections affect the distribution of the numbers of Black and White men incarcerated at each education level, Pettit calculates dramatic comparative "cumulative risks of imprisonment" for Black men in particular on the basis of her emended educational attainment rates:[4]

Cumulative Risk of Imprisonment by Ages 30 to 34

All		Less Than High School		High School/GED		Some College	
White	Black	White	Black	White	Black	White	Black
5.4	28.0	28.0	68.0	6.2	21.4	1.2	6.6

We can look at this on an annual, rather than cumulative, basis. In 2008, for example, when of the approximately 4.2 million African-American men ages 20-34, approximately 1.6 million had not completed high school, thirty-seven percent of those men were incarcerated; by ages 35-40, 40% will have been incarcerated. Most by that point will have at least two children of their own, left to be raised in poverty by a "female householder" living in racially and economically isolated neighborhoods with few resources. Just over a quarter of White men who lack a high school diploma risk spending time in prison by age 34. The risk for Black men is more than two out of three. While the probability of imprisonment for African-American men with some college is approximately the same as that for White men with just a high school diploma or GED, that for White men with some college is insignificant. An African-American man who is able to complete some college reduces his risk of imprisonment by 90%.

However, this is only half the story. The pipelines flow in both directions and to a large extent "the prison to school pipeline" is the more important. Much of the reason for the lack of educational achievement by many Black children follows from the extraordinary rates at which their fathers are arrested by police and incarcerated with the complicity of prosecutors and judges. Imprisoned men can contribute little or nothing to save their children from lives spent in poverty. Even formerly imprisoned men all too often have little chance of finding work that can support their children above the poverty level, particularly given their own usual lack of effective educational attainment. As housing patterns are strongly associated with household income, the families of incarcerated or formerly incarcerated men, especially if they are African-American, are among the most likely to live in neighborhoods of concentrated poverty.

In addition, because of the increasing segregation of American cities, it is much more likely that a middle class Black family than a middle class White family will be forced to live in a neighborhood of concentrated poverty, simply by virtue of their race. (The oddity of the idea that a middle class White family would be unable to find a home outside an area of concentrated poverty points to the racist nature of American housing patterns.) Schools in segregated neighborhoods of concentrated poverty are usually inadequate to their mission. A Black student in an integrated suburban school — without regard to that student's family income — can be as much as six times more likely to graduate on-time and college-ready than a Black student in a segregated urban school. Similarly, a Black student in a segregated urban school, even a Black student from a middle class family, is unlikely to receive an education that will graduate him from high school on-time and college- or career-ready.

Concentrated neighborhood poverty, because of the peculiarities of the drug laws and matters at the level of detail of police officer reward systems and the political ambitions of district attorneys, leads to disproportionately intense police activity and prosecutions in predominately Black neighborhoods. Quite apart from this, or, more exactly, in addition to this, neighborhoods of concentrated poverty in themselves foster high rates of violent felonies. High rates of incarceration of young Black men lead to high rates of concentrated poverty for their neighborhoods, where ineffective schools contribute to high rates of incarceration and poverty, which foster high rates of violent offensives, and so on and on. The combination of these factors put astonishing numbers of young adult Black men at risk of incarceration and give another turn to the wheel of disadvantage for their children.

Most people, particularly most African-Americans, are familiar with this situation. The question is, then, what is to be done to end disproportionate Black poverty?

The response to the question is frequently a resort to the American doctrine of individual responsibility. Issues of culture, community and psychology are, no doubt, important contributors to the achievement gap in education as well as to the disparities in incarceration rates. However, it is unclear whether they are causes or consequences. We are told that young Black men should pull up their socks (and their trousers) and simply do better in school and act better in the community. Examples of "beating the odds" and "resiliency" are featured by the media, foundations, community groups and inspirational speakers. These responses are simultaneously positive and negative ways of blaming the victims of racism and each in their own manner is a way of maintaining the system of racism. On the other hand, as we have seen, institutional policy decisions are clearly causal, definable and quantifiable and, possibly, given the public will, amenable to change. The goal, after all, is not for individuals to beat the odds. The goal is to change the odds, or, rather, to change the game.

How is that to be done?

As we have seen, there are many possible leverage points. One of the most obvious is that of disparate rates of incarceration for drug offenses, the contemporary equivalent of the vagrancy laws of the Jim Crow era. There are few who now defend laws prohibiting the private use of drugs like marijuana and the police practices associated with them. Why not change them? As we have seen, hundreds of thousands of young Black and Hispanic men are unlawfully arrested each year for purported marijuana offenses alone. To these may be added those incarcerated Black men who would not be incarcerated, or would not be incarcerated for such lengthy periods, if it were not due to the remaining disparate effects of arrests and sentencing for crack and powder cocaine and other drug offenses. Calculating a projected number of adult Black drug arrests (including both possession and sales) based on the drug arrest rate for White adults (given that the actual criminalized activity is roughly equivalent), we found that the difference between this projection and actual arrests, on average, is nearly 350,000 arrests of Black adults annually beyond the amount to be expected based on the actually equivalent drug use rates of Blacks and Whites. We can, then, work from a nominal figure of 100,000 excessive incarcerations of young adult Black men annually from inequitable drug abuse arrests. A reasonable estimate would be an annual loss to the Black community of $2 billion dollars in income. If 60,000 of those incarcerated Black men are fathers, ending disparities in drug abuse arrests could well lower the number of Black children living in poverty by something approaching that figure. Or, to put it another way, each year perhaps 60,000 Black children would not be condemned to living in poverty: 400,000 over five years, if laws like those recently adopted in the states of Washington and Colorado were applied nationally.[†]

Or we could begin by ending disparities in school funding or, better yet, move to "challenge-based" funding formulae, such as that developed for the Abbott districts in New Jersey. This would raise male Black high school graduation rates nationally to approximately the level of male White rates. The national high school graduation rate for male White students is 78%, that for male Black students is 52%. But many suburban districts graduate male Black students at rates similar to the national graduation rates of male White students. Three large districts near Washington, D.C., do so. One, Fairfax County, Virginia, has achieved a graduation rate for male Black students of 80%. Nationally, with approximately 360,000 Black male students in ninth grade, closing the gap will produce 94,000 more male Black high school graduates each year. As incarceration rates vary with educational attainment, this will result in a lower incarceration rate for African-

---

[†] Is it significant that these are states with relatively low percentages of African-American residents? States where the drug laws primarily affect White people?

American men and higher incomes for both incarcerated and free Black men.

Here are some other, more detailed, if still "back of the envelope," estimates:

The incarceration rate for Black men, ages twenty to thirty-four, without a high school diploma was 37.2% in 2008, according to Betty Pettit, while for those with a high school diploma was 9.1%. We will estimate the incarceration rate of those with some college at just over 2% and that of those with a Bachelor's degree or higher slightly less. At a high school graduation rate of 52%, we would expect 64,300 of those not graduating to be incarcerated, 11,500 of those with a high school diploma and no further education and 1,300 of those with some college and 1,200 with a Bachelor's degree or higher: a total of 78,000 of the cohort of 360,000. At a high school graduation rate of 78%, we would expect 29,000 of those not graduating to be incarcerated, 12,800 of the larger number of those with a high school diploma and no further education, 2,900 of those with some college and 1,200 of those attaining a Bachelor's degree or higher: a total of 46,000: nearly 32,000 fewer.

That is the education improvement incarceration subtotal. We can then estimate the economic effects of closing the high school graduation gap. Average incomes, like incarceration rates, vary with educational attainment. In 2006 The College Board calculated the distributions shown on the next chart.

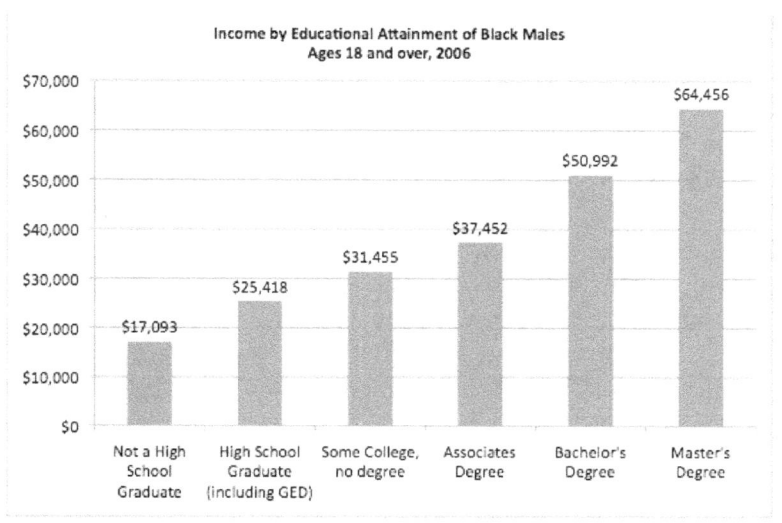

Income by Educational Attainment of Black Males
Ages 18 and over, 2006

As, unfortunately, there has been little change in incomes over the past few years, these figures will do for our estimates. Averaging incomes for "Some College, no degree" and "Associates Degree" and those for Bachelor's and Master's degrees, we can arrive at estimates of total income figures for each level of educational attainment for our grade 9 cohort once they complete schooling, deducting the numbers incarcerated at each level of educational attainment for each graduation rate. At the current graduation rate of 52%, those not graduating and not incarcerated, as a group, would be expected to earn $4.5 billion per year; those with a high school diploma and no further qualifications $1.9 billion; those with some college (estimated by doubling the number of those with an Associate's degree), $2.4 billion and those with a Bachelor's degree or higher $4.7 billion, for a total of $13.5 billion. At a high school graduation rate of 78%, the corresponding figures would be $850 million, $6.7 billion, $3.7 billion and $7.1 billion, for a total of $18.4 billion: an increase of $4.9 billion or 36%.

This difference in incarceration rates and incomes of young adult Black men would of course tend to alleviate overall Black childhood poverty. Forty-five percent of the 2.4 million Black children under the age of 18 living with their mother with no husband present now live in poverty. If we assume two children per family unit, we can estimate just under half a million women and just over a million children in this category. These are numbers approximating those that would be arrived at by basing an estimate on the number of incarcerated Black men. Given that over half of all prisoners have children under the age of 18,[5] the reduction in incarcerations resulting from closing the high school graduation gap would reduce the number of those households by 16,000 and the number of children living in poverty by 32,000 each year—about 3%.

We might, for the sake of this illustration, add the benefits of ending drug law disparate incarcerations to those of closing the high school graduation gap.[‡] Our running total, then, would be approaching $7 billion annually in increased income for the Black community and 90,000 Black children removed from poverty, or $35 billion in increased income and 450,000 Black children removed from poverty over five years. This would have a compounding effect on the increase in the educational attainment level of Black children as many of their families would no longer forced to live in neighborhoods of concentrated poverty.

At this point we can look at the effects of the mass incarceration of African-American men from another angle. According to the Bureau of Labor Statistics, there were 47 million White, non-Hispanic, men and 35 million White, non-Hispanic women employed full time in the third quarter of 2012. In other words, 57% of the White, non-Hispanic, workforce was male. Similar gender ratios held for Hispanic and Asian workers. But there were 5.4 million male Black workers and 6.2 million Black female workers: just 47% of the Black workforce was male. In all groups, despite the law and generations of effort, men were paid more than women. The

---

[‡] The incarceration rates for African-American men for drug offenses do not appear to vary with educational attainment.

median Black weekly wages were $633 for men and $590 for women. (As a matter of interest, median wages for White women were $712, for White men, $854.) If we assume that the gender wage differential remains the same, the total weekly wage deficit for the Black community would be $500 million if equal percentages of Black men and women were employed and $895 million if the number of Black men employed were 110 percent of the number of Black women in full-time employment. Bearing in mind that there are nearly 900,000 African-American men in prison, the number of additional Black male workers at parity would be 793,000; at 110% it would be 1.4 million. If we assume a 48-week working year (two weeks of vacation and ten days of customary holidays), the annual income differential for the Black community as a whole would be between $24 and $43 billion.

It was noted earlier that Black men are incarcerated for violent crimes more often than for drug offenses. The potential for reducing the number of incarcerated Black men is, therefore, even greater than for those incarcerated for drug offenses if the size of this group can be reduced. While the disproportionate incarceration of Black men for drug offenses can be traced to the operations of law enforcement, that for violent crimes appears to be an artifact (as well as a cause) of poverty. There is a large scholarly literature exploring the link between poverty and violent crime and it is well-established that as poverty goes up (or down) rates of violent crime move nearly in parallel, at least to a "saturation point" of poverty, beyond which crime rates appear to level off.[6] It is not that there is a link between specifically Black poverty and violent crime (or between African-Americans per se and violent crime, as was held by segregationists), it is that reductions in neighborhood poverty appear to produce similar reductions in violent crime in both White and Black neighborhoods.[§]

[§] It remains possible that residential segregation may produce similarities between Black middle-class and high-poverty areas in terms of crime rates, simply because segregation causes such neighborhoods to be in close physical proximity to one another.

We can approximate the national violent crime rate for Black men with reference to the New York State data discussed earlier. Here again is the table of New York State incarcerations by type of offense:

Crime	White Prisoners	Black Prisoners	Hispanic Prisoners	Total
Violent Felony	7,005	18,505	8,892	34,402
Other Coercive	1,459	1,871	927	4,257
Drug Offenses	938	3,883	2,206	7,027
Property and Other	3,261	2,319	1,154	6,734
Youth & Juvenile	229	628	252	1,109
Total	12,892	27,211	13,431	53,534

New York State's Black violent crime incarceration rate is ten times that of the White violent crime incarceration rate (0.06% of the White population is incarcerated for violent offenses vs. 0.6% of the Black population). Approximately two-thirds of Black prisoners were incarcerated for violent felonies. If we assume an association of 80% between changes in poverty rates and changes in violent offensive rates, then a decline of 4% in the poverty rate would bring a decline of 3.2% in the number of incarcerations of Black men for violent offenses in New York, or just under 19,000. Over five years that would be approximately 93,000 fewer incarcerated Black men in New York State. With over 800,000 incarcerated Black men,[**] nationally, a similar effect would reduce that number by 33,600 annually, increasing the income of the Black community by over $650 million each year: 168,000 fewer prisoners over five years, $3.25 billion in increased income for each 4% decline in the poverty rate.

[**] "Correctional Facilities for Adults," 2010 Census Summary File 2.

*   *   *

Again: What is to be done? And who is to do it?

The most straightforward beginning point for reducing Black poverty is the elimination of disparities in arrests and incarcerations for drug offences and other issues giving rise to inequities of a similar kind, such as trespass. This can be accomplished by relatively uncomplicated administrative measures: agreements among the key decision makers in the local, state and federal criminal justice systems to end the policies and practices that cause those disparities. An example of such good practice is the decision by the district attorney in the Bronx, New York City, to stop prosecuting young men arrested for trespass while standing in front of their own apartment doors.†† Police, with the cooperation of citizen's groups, could devise equitable formulas for the allocation of effort and to test whether activities and arrests were racially disproportionate. District attorneys and prosecutors could devise similar procedures. Judges could be more sensitive to racial disparities in the cases brought before them and the sentences asked for by prosecutors as well as during jury selection processes. All decision-makers in the criminal justice system should move immediately to halt the criminalization of school discipline matters.

Improving educational attainment for male Black students can be accomplished. It has been accomplished in the Washington, D.C., suburbs and other suburban school systems across the country and by the Abbott efforts in New Jersey, by investments in early childhood education, extended school time, equitable school discipline policies and the professional development of educators. In the long run, this would be facilitated most efficiently by changing the basis of school funding from neighborhood property tax to some wider basis,

---

†† This decision has been followed by one by Judge Shira A. Scheindlin of Federal District Court in Manhattan that the practice is unconstitutional.

such as a state's general revenue. However, it is not necessary to wait for the outcome of what would no doubt be a complicated political process to accomplish this. Some states have already approximated a similar result by varying state aid in inverse proportion to local revenue. In this way a state might, for example, determine the average per student expenditure of the wealthiest quintile of districts and distribute school aid so that all districts in the state are "averaged up" to that level. Intra-district funding disparities can be remedied administratively at the district level, as can intra-district programming disparities, such as the distribution of gifted and talented programs, course offerings and the like. Racial disparities in out-of-school suspensions are another issue that can be addressed at the school and district level.

It is important to level the playing field and shocking that in much of the country it is routine that educational resources are directed away from those most in need of them. But as the research behind New Jersey's Abbott school funding case showed, children whose families are not well-educated must have additional resources if they are to finish their schooling career and college ready. The resources must be there so that they arrive at first grade ready to learn to read. Resources for challenging elementary and secondary curricula must be in place as well as for the extended education time enjoyed by the children of wealthier families: more learning time each day; more learning days in each week and more learning time during the summer. This must be combined with continually professional development for their teachers, both in subject area knowledge and teaching skills.

Implementing the E.E.O.C. guidance to employers in regard to the hiring of formerly incarcerated African-American men and educational and training programs at community colleges can increase the income of African-American neighborhoods where there is currently concentrated poverty. These can begin with GED classes, and continue through Associates degrees and employment skills training programs coordinated with local employers. ("Green training" is one example of a promising type of program offered by community colleges, such as LaGuardia Community College in New York City.)

Combining programs to improve educational attainment for Black male students and to eliminate of disparate rates of incarceration for matters such as drug offenses would cause the poverty rate for Black children to decline significantly and the income of the Black community to increase. As the Black community's income increased, the rate of violent offenses and incarcerations for those would decrease, further increasing the community's income and educational attainment. Disparate Black poverty would begin to come to an end.

Taken together these recommendations are a minimal agenda for the world's dominant nation. Resources are not the issue. The issue is whether we have the will to challenge historic prejudices and a heritage of injustice.

Notes

---

[1] Myrdal, Gunner, An American Dilemma, p. 75, in Cox, Oliver C. Caste, Class and Race: A Study in Social Dynamics. New York: Modern Reader, 1970 (1948), p. 521.

[2] Pettit, Becky. Invisible Men: Mass Incarceration and the Myth of Black Progress. New York: Russell Sage Foundation, 2011, pp. 68-9.

[3] Pettit, p. 7.

[4] Pettit, p. 17.

[5] "Over half of all prisoners have children under the age of 18, and about 45 percent of those parents were living with their children at the time they were sent to prison." (Incarceration and Social Inequality. Bruce Western and Becky Pettit, January 2010, p. 11) http://projects.iq.harvard.edu/prisonstudiesproject/files/Incarceration_and_Social_Inequality.pdf

[6] See especially: Hannon, Lance, and Robert DeFina. "Violent Crime In African American and White Neighborhoods: Is Poverty's Detrimental Effect Race-Specific?" and Hipp, John R. and Yates, Daniel K., "Ghettos, Thresholds, and Crime: Does Concentrated Poverty Really have an Accelerating Increasing Effect on Crime" Criminology, Volume 49, Number 4, 2011, pp. 955 ff.

Bibliography

Alexander, Michelle. The New Jim Crow: Mass Incarceration in the Age of Colorblindness. The New Press: New York, 2010.

Baker, Bruce, David Sciarra and Danielle Farrie. Is School Funding Fair? A National Report Card. Education Law Center, New Jersey. Second edition: June 2012.

Bishaw, Alemayehu. Areas with Concentrated Poverty: 2006-2010. American Community Survey Briefs, December, 2011.

Blackmon, Douglas A. Slavery by Another Name: The Re-Enslavement of Black Americans from the Civil War to World War II. New York: Doubleday, 2008.

Bureau of Labor Statistics, Establishment Data, Historical Employment, Table B-1. Employment on nonfarm payrolls by major industry sector, 1962 to date. ftp://ftp.bls.gov/pub/suppl/empsit.ceseeb1.txt

Cox, Oliver C. Caste, Class and Race: A Study in Social Dynamics. New York: Modern Reader, 1970.

De los Santos, Barbur I. and Heckman, James J. Prevalence of Prison GED Recipiency and Implications for Labor Market Outcomes and Recividism. May 11, 2005

DeFina, Robert and Lance Hannon The Impact of Mass Incarceration on Poverty

DeFina, Robert H. and Lance Hannon. "The Impact of Adult Incarceration on Child Poverty: A County-Level Analysis, 1995-2007." The Prison Journal 2010 90: 377 originally published online 9 September 2010 DOI: 10.1177/0032885510382085. The online version of this article can be found at: http://tpj.sagepub.com/content/90/4/377, p. 16.

Du Bois, W. E. B. Black Reconstruction in America, 1860-1880. New York: Free Press, 1999.

Editorial. "Examining Marijuana Arrests," The New York Times, April 1, 2012.

Ellen, Ingrid Gould and Horn, Keren Mertens. Do Federally Assisted Households Have Access to High Performing Public Schools. Poverty & Race Research Action Council. Civil Rights Research, November 2012.

Equal Employment Opportunity Commission. "Consideration of Arrest and Conviction Records in Employment Decisions Under Title VII of the Civil Rights Act of 1964." See: www.eeoc.gov/laws/guidance/arrest_conviction.cfm#sdend note65sym

Fabelo, Tony et al., Breaking Schools' Rules: A Statewide Study of How School Discipline Relates to Students' Success and Juvenile Justice Involvement. 2011

Fagan, Jeffrey, Valerie West, and Jan Holland. Reciprocal Effects of Crime and Incarceration in New York City Neighborhoods. Fordham Urban Law Journal, Volume 30, Issue 5, 2002.

Federal Bureau of Investigation. "Crime in the United States 2010," FBI Uniform Crime Report (Washington, DC: US Dept. of Justice, September 2011).

Fitzhugh, George, The Blessings of Slavery in http://www.teachingamericanhistory.org/library/index.asp? documentprint=2597

Gallman, Robert E. Trends in the Size Distribution of Wealth in the Nineteenth Century: Some Speculations, in Soltow, Lee, ed. Six Papers on the Size Distribution of Wealth and Income, NBER, 1969.

Gelman, Andrew, Fagan, Jeffrey, and Alex Kiss. An Analysis of the New York City Police Department's "Stop-and-Frisk" Policy in the Context of Claims of Racial Bias. Journal of the American Statistical Association September 2007, Vol. 102, No. 479, Applications and Case Studies.

Gilliam, W. S. (2005). Prekindergarteners left behind: Expulsion rates in state prekindergarten systems. New Haven, CT: Yale University Child Study Center.

Glaze, Lauren E. Correctional Population in the United States, 2010. U.S. Department of Justice, Office of Justice Programs, Bureau of Justice Statistics, December 2011, NCJ 236319.

Glaze, Lauren E. and Bonczar, Thomas P. Probation and Parole in the United States, 2010. U.S. Department of Justice, Office of Justice Programs, Bureau of Justice Statistics, November 2011, NCJ 236019.

Hannon, Lance and Robert DeFina. "Violent Crime In African-American And White Neighborhoods: Is Poverty's Detrimental Effect Race-Specific?" http://www88.homepage.villanova.edu/lance.hannon/ Forthcoming%20in%20the%20Journal%20of%20Pove rty.pdf accessed 06/15/12

Hannon, Lance, and Robert DeFina. "Violent Crime In African American and White Neighborhoods: Is Poverty's Detrimental Effect Race-Specific?"

Harris, Angel L. Kids Don't Want to Fail: Oppositional Culture and the Black-White Achievement Gap. Cambridge, Massachusetts: Harvard University Press, 2011.

Harry Levine & Deborah Small, N.Y. Civil Liberties Union, Marijuana Arrest Crusade: Racial Bias and Police Policy In New York City, 1997""2007, at 13""16 (2008), www.nyclu.org/files/MARIJUANA-ARREST-CRUSADE_Final.pdf

Hernandez, Donald J. Double Jeopardy: How Third-Grade Reading Skills and Poverty Influence High School Graduation. The Annie E. Casey Foundation, April 2011.

Heuer, Ruth and Stephanie Stullich. Comparability of State and Local Expenditures Among Schools Within Districts: A Report from the Study of School-Level Expenditures. U.S. Department of Education, Office of Planning, Evaluation and Policy Development, Policy and Program Studies Service, 2011, p. 29.

Hilferty, Fiona, The Implications of Poverty on Children's Readiness to Learn. Australian Rsearch Alliance for Children & Youth, 2009.

Hipp, John R. and Yates, Daniel K., "Ghettos, Thresholds, and Crime: Does Concentrated Poverty Really have an Accelerating Increasing Effect on Crime" Criminology, Volume 49, Number 4, 2011, pp. 955 ff.

Human Rights Watch, Decades of Disparity: Drug Arrests and Race in the United States 1 (2009), http://www.hrw.org/sites/default/files/reports/us0309web_1.pdf

Incarceration and Social Inequality. Bruce Western and Becky Pettit January 2010, p. 11) http://projects.iq.harvard.edu/prisonstudiesproject/files/Incarceration_and_Social_Inequality.pdf

Johnson, Rucker C. Intergenerational Risks of Criminal Involvement and Incarceration. April 2007.

Lewis, Sharon; Simon, Candace; Uzzell, Renata; Horwitz, Amanda; Casserly, Michael. A Call for Change: The Social and Educational Factors Contributing to the Outcomes of Black Males in Urban Schools. Council of Great City Schools, October, 2010.

Lopoo, Leonard and DeLeire, Thomas. Pursuing the American Dream: Economic Mobility Across Generations. Pew Charitable Trusts, 2012.

Myrdal, Gunnar. An American Dilemma: The Negro Problem and Modern Democracy. New York: Harper & Brothers Publishers, 1944.

Oliver, Pamela E. Gary Sandefur, Jessica Jakubowski, and James E. Yocom. The Effect of Black Male Imprisonment on Black Child Poverty.

Ooms, Herman. Tokugawa Village Practice: Class, Status, Power, Law. Berkeley: University of California Press, 1996.

Orfield, G. and Lee, C. (2005). Why segregation matters: Poverty and educational inequality. Cambridge, MA: The Civil Rights Project at Harvard University.

Orfield, John Kucsera and Genevieve Siegel-Hawley. E Pluribus . . . Separation: Deepening Double Segregation for More Students. The Civil Rights Project, September 2012.

Pettit, Becky. Invisible Men: Mass Incarceration and the Myth of Black Progress. New York: Russell Sage Foundation, 2011.

Rivera, Ray. "Pockets of City See Higher Use of Force During Police Stops." The New York Times, August 16, 2012 and Associated Press. "U.S. Justice Department Alleges Violations of Students' Rights in Meridian, Miss., Schools." The Times-Picayune, August 10, 2012.

Rothwell, Jonathan. Housing Costs, Zoning, and Access to High-Scoring Schools. Brookings Institution, April 2012. http://www.brookings.edu/~/media/Files/rc/papers/2012/04 19_school_inequality_rothwell/0419_school_inequality_rot hwell.pdf

Rumberger, Russell W. Parsing the Data on Student Achievement in High-Poverty Schools. North Carolina Law Review, 85 (2007).

Schott Foundation for Public Education. A Rotting Apple: Education Redlining in New York City, 2011.

Schott Foundation for Public Education. The Urgency of Now: The 2012 Schott 50 State Report on Public Education and Black Males.

Spatig-Amerikaner, Ary. Unequal Education: Federal Loophole Enables Lower Spending on Students of Color. Center for American Progress, August 2012.

Speri, Alice. "2010 Marijuana Arrests Top 1978-96 Total," New York Times, February 11, 2011.

Stiglitz, Joseph E. The Price of Inequality. London: W. W. Norton & Company, 2012.

Stuntz, William J. The Collapse of American Criminal Justice. Harvard University Press, 2011.

U.S. Department of Health & Human Services, Substance Abuse & Mental Health Services. Administration. Results from the 2010 National Survey on Drug Use and Health: Summary of National Findings 21 (2011),

http://oas.samhsa.gov/NSDUH/2k10NSDUH/2k10Results.
    pdf

Western, Bruce. Punishment and Inequality in America. New
    York: Russell Sage Foundation, 2006.

Western, Bruce. "Interview with Bruce Western." Social
    Thought and Research, Volume 30 (2009).
    http://hdl.handle.net/1808/5697

Western, Dr. Bruce and Dr. Becky Pettit. Collateral Costs:
    Incarceration's Effect on Economic Mobility. Washington,
    DC: The Pew Charitable Trusts, 2010.

Index

A

B

C

D

E

www.ingramcontent.com/pod-product-compliance
Lightning Source LLC
Chambersburg PA
CBHW070647290526
45790CB00001B/218